W. Goddard

HANDBOOK TO
THE ROMAN WALL

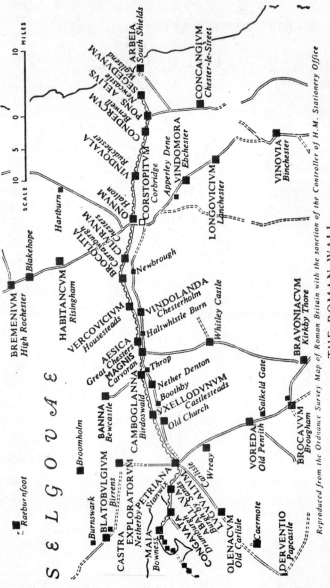

THE ROMAN WALL

Reproduced from the Ordnance Survey Map of Roman Britain with the sanction of the Controller of H.M. Stationery Office

SELGOVAE

ARBEIA
South Shields

CONCANGIVM
Chester-le-Street

SEGEDVNVM
Wallsend

PONS AELIVS
Newcastle

CONDERCVM
Benwell

VINDOMORA
Ebchester

VINOVIA
Binchester

VINDOVALA
Rudchester

Apperley Dene

CORSTOPITVM
Corbridge

LONGOVICIVM
Lanchester

ONNVM
Halton

CILVRNVM
Chesters

BROCOLITIA
Carrawburgh

Newbrough

VINDOLANDA
Chesterholm

VERCOVICIVM
Housesteads

Haltwhistle Burn

Whitley Castle

BRAVONIACVM
Kirkby Thore

AESICA
Great Chesters

MAGNIS
Carvoran

Throp

Nether Denton

Boothby

VXELLODVNVM
Castlesteads

Salkeld Gate

VOREDA
Old Penrith

BROCAVVM
Brougham

BANNA
Bewcastle

CAMBOGLANNA
Birdoswald

Old Church

Broomholm

Raeburnfoot

Burnswark

BLATOBVLGIVM
Birrens

CASTRA
EXPLORATORVM
Netherby

PETRIANA
Stanwix

MAIA
Bowness

Carlisle

Wreay

Caermote

OLENACVM
Old Carlisle

DERVENTIO
Papcastle

BREMENIVM
High Rochester

HABITANCVM
Risingham

Blakehope

Hariburn

MILES
10

SCALE

HANDBOOK TO
THE ROMAN WALL

J. COLLINGWOOD BRUCE
LL.D., D.C.L., F.S.A.

Twelfth Edition

EDITED BY

SIR IAN RICHMOND

Sole Trade Distributors

HAROLD HILL & SON LIMITED

NEWCASTLE UPON TYNE

HINDSON & ANDREW REID LTD

1966

First Published 1863
Second Edition 1884
Third Edition 1885
Fourth Edition 1895
Fifth Edition 1907
Sixth Edition 1909
Seventh Edition 1914
Eighth Edition 1921: Reprinted 1925 and 1927
Ninth Edition 1933: Reprinted 1937
Tenth Edition 1947: Reprinted 1951
Eleventh Edition 1957
Extensively Revised by Sir Ian Richmond
Twelfth Edition 1965: Reprinted 1970

S.B.N. 902407 015

© Hindson & Andrew Reid Ltd. 1966

PRINTED IN ENGLAND BY HINDSON & ANDREW REID LTD
AT STRAWBERRY HOUSE, NEWCASTLE UPON TYNE

CONTENTS

CHAPTER I

CHAPTER II

CHAPTER III

CONTENTS — *continued*

MAPS

PREFACE TO THE TWELFTH EDITION

" John Collingwood Bruce was born in 1805 and, after graduating at Glasgow, became a schoolmaster in Newcastle upon Tyne. During the whole of a long and active life, until his death in 1892, he was an untiring student of Roman antiquities, and especially of the great Wall with which his memory will always be associated. Even more valuable than his work as a field archaeologist, however, were his services to the study of Roman inscriptions. He had the qualities of an epigraphist to an eminent degree: patience, pertinacity, a quick eye and a retentive memory were so combined in him with sound scholarship, that for many years he was the leading authority on Roman inscriptions in this country; and the British volume of the Berlin *Corpus Inscriptionum Latinarum* consists mainly of material which he supplied. His *Handbook of the Roman Wall* was first written in 1863, when the materials for the definitive edition of his great book on *The Roman Wall* were practically complete."

The foregoing words, from the preface to the late Professor Collingwood's Ninth Edition, are an authoritative estimate of Dr. Bruce's work by one pre-eminently qualified to make it. The present editor's task, on the basis laid by these scholars, is to bring their work up to date, by inclusion of new discoveries and of references to them in the bibliography. This task has been immeasurably facilitated by Professor Eric Birley's *Research on Hadrian's Wall* (1961). Most of the old illustrations have been retained, but several drawn by the editor have been added or substituted. The Society of Antiquaries of Newcastle upon Tyne has kindly permitted the use of the illustrations on pages 52, 53, 62, 74, 92, 94, 104, 130 and 142; the Cumberland and Westmorland Antiquarian and Archaeological Society of those on pages 162, 170, 171, 173, 178, 182, 188, 200, 202, 204, and 208, and the Clarendon Press of that on page 114.

It has also seemed that the wording of 1863, and even some of the sentiments of that time, had by 1963 become so dated and even so distasteful that some revision of the diction was required. But the closing paragraph of Professor Collingwood's preface is used a third time to close this one, not only out of love and respect for him but because it echoes so well the fitness of things concerning a Wall pilgrimage.

" A book like this has the singular privilege of not lying still all its days indoors, but travelling with its owner and sharing his fortunes of wind and weather. The privilege is doubly precious when the journey itself is a notable one, and those who have made it are agreed that there is something more than notable about the pilgrimage of the Wall. It is the editor's dearest wish that this book may long continue to accompany those who make that pilgrimage, honourably scarred and stained in their service; that it may remind them how many have travelled the Wall before them and have earned the right to say, with Camden, ' Verily I have seene the tract of it over the high pitches and steepe descents of hilles, wonderfully rising and falling '; and that it may strengthen in them the will that these relics and this pilgrimage should be preserved for our posterity as part of their national heritage."

I. A. R.

Oxford,
1965.

HANDBOOK TO

THE ROMAN WALL

CHAPTER I

INTRODUCTORY

A VISITOR to the Roman Wall who has a thorough love of antiquity and appreciates the importance of the monument will wish to know something of the authors who have written about the Wall and its history.

I EARLIER ACCOUNTS

The first important account is by William Camden, the great Elizabethan antiquary, written in 1599 and printed in the fifth edition (1600) of his *Britannia*. Camden himself visited the Wall; but not its central part, because of the danger of robbers. He advanced a complete and logical explanation of the Wall and its works which, though now superseded, held the field for 250 years.

The *Britannia*, written in Latin, was Englished in 1610 by Philemon Holland, in consultation with Camden; and Henry Holland, his son, produced a new edition in 1637. The Holland translations long remained standard works on the archaeology of Britain, and passed through many revisions, notably those by Bishop Gibson (1695, 1722, 1753, 1772) and Richard Gough (1789, 1806). Gibson's later editions contain results of a fresh examination of the Wall in 1708-9 and, for the first time, an account of the whole line. Gough is based upon John Horsley (1685-1732), Presbyterian minister and schoolmaster at Morpeth, endowed with learning, industry, and judgment. Horsley's *Britannia Romana*,

1

published in 1732 after his death, is still a prime treatise on
the Roman antiquities of Britain; and his account of the
Wall is most careful and penetrating. His materials were
used, unacknowledged, by Alexander Gordon in *Itinerarium
Septentrionale* (1726). A plagiarised version of Horsley's
description of the Wall was also Warburton's *Vallum
Romanum* of 1753.

William Stukeley's *Iter Boreale*, published in 1776 and
also posthumous, includes memoranda of a journey made
in 1725 with Roger Gale, over western and northern
England. It contained a new theory of the relation between
Wall and Vallum, and drawings most useful in showing the
state of the remains in his time. Another short first-hand
account of the Wall came from John Brand, in an appendix
to the first volume of his *History of Newcastle* (1789).

William Hutton of Birmingham, at the age of 78, walked
the Wall from end to end in 1801 and recorded his en-
thusiastic observations in *The History of the Roman Wall*.
Six years later, the Rev. Dr. John Lingard walked from
Wallsend to Gilsland, making manuscript notes entitled
Mural Tourification, largely transcribed in 1929 by R. C.
Bosanquet. The fourth volume of *Magna Britannia* (1816),
by Daniel and Samuel Lysons, contained an article on the
Wall and a good account of Roman inscriptions in Cumber-
land.

Meanwhile, the Rev. John Hodgson, then incumbent of
Jarrow and Heworth, had written *The Picture of Newcastle
upon Tyne* (1812), with a comprehensive and useful account
of the Wall; and in 1839 devoted a large part of the last
volume of his *History of Northumberland* to the Walls of
Hadrian and Antoninus. Everyone since Camden had viewed
the Vallum as Hadrian's frontier-work and the Wall as that
of Severus; Hodgson saw that the evidence of inscriptions
made this untenable; and he regarded Wall and Vallum as
contemporary and the Vallum as a rearward defence, an
idea partly anticipated by Stukeley.

Twelve years later came Bruce's *Roman Wall*, first
edition, 1851; second 1853; third 1867. The last edition, a

fine quarto, is a detailed description of the remains, excellent
in the east and centre, less good in the west, with accounts
of Roman sites near the Wall, inscriptions and other objects;
also an important short chapter on the question of who
built the Wall. Bruce's work summarised the results of
excavation by John Clayton of Chesters and publicised
Hodgson's theory of Hadrianic date. Bruce also produced the
valuable *Lapidarium Septentrionale* in 1870-1875, which,
contemporary with the *Corpus Inscriptionum Latinarum*,
vol. VII, edited by Hübner in 1873, gave full versions of the
inscriptions. Since then, inscriptions up to 1954 have been
published by R. G. Collingwood and R. P. Wright in *Roman
Inscriptions of Britain* (1965) and annually from 1921 in the
Journal of Roman Studies. In 1858 the first accurate survey
of the Wall, *A Survey of the Roman Wall*, was made by
Henry MacLauchlan in the years 1852-1854 for the third
Duke of Northumberland, with an explanatory *Memoir*. In
1964 the Ordnance Survey published a magnificent special
archaeological map of *Hadrian's Wall*, at a scale of 2 inches
to the mile, which marks and differentiates upstanding and
buried remains and which anyone visiting the Wall will find
invaluable.

Twentieth-century excavation on the Wall is published in
Archaeologia Aeliana by the Society of Antiquaries of New-
castle upon Tyne, or in the Cumberland and Westmorland
Archaeological and Antiquarian Society's *Transactions*.
Summaries of main conclusions have appeared in the *Journal
of Roman Studies*, in articles called *Hadrian's Wall, a history
of the problem* (1920); *Hadrian's Wall, 1921-1930* (1931);
The Turf Wall of Hadrian 1895-1935 (1935); and *Hadrian's
Wall, 1939-1949* (1950). The *Northumberland County History*
has published descriptions of the Wall from Wallsend to
Rudchester Burn (vol. XIII).

II HISTORICAL SUMMARY

Britain was known to both Greeks and Romans by the
fourth century B.C.; but first came into touch with Roman
military power when Julius Caesar invaded it in 55 and

54 B.C. These were mere raids: conquest was reserved for Claudius in A.D. 43. But it was a generation later when Roman troops first penetrated the northern regions. Julius Agricola, governor of Britain from 78 to 85, occupied all the north of England and Scotland to the fringe of the Highlands; the districts he had conquered were studded with forts and lined with roads dominating lines of movement and isolating native communities. One of these roads was that known in medieval times as the Stanegate, linking Corbridge with Carlisle.

Agricola's northernmost schemes of consolidation were never completely realised. His successors held Scotland south of the Earn until not long after the turn of the century. After the abandonment of Scotland the situation worsened and became acute at the close of Trajan's reign. It was then that the new Emperor, Hadrian, visiting Britain in 122, decided to build a Wall from Tyne to Solway so as to create a continuous and permanent frontier barrier. This is the Wall of which the present volume gives some account: it marks the apogee of the system of cordon control.

The Emperor did not remain in the province to see the execution of the Wall, and it was Aulus Platorius Nepos, governor of Britain from 122 until at least 126, who carried them forward and began to modify them; the final touches came some years after A.D. 130. There is much evidence in the developing design of the works that their construction was bitterly resented, because of the iron frontier-control which they imposed.

Antoninus Pius succeeded Hadrian in 138. In the next year, preparations began, under Lollius Urbicus, for a fresh advance into Scotland, consolidated by a new outer Wall between Forth and Clyde. For a time Hadrian's Wall was less strongly held. Peace was restless and precarious; there were tumults in 155-8 and in 162, during the first of which the northern Wall was evacuated and after which Hadrian's Wall was again strongly held: and in 181, under Commodus invaders again crossed the northern Wall, which was repaired under Ulpius Marcellus and soon abandoned for ever.

Commodus was assassinated at the end of 192, and there followed a struggle for the Empire, in which Septimius Severus was ultimately triumphant. The strongest claimant was Clodius Albinus, governor of Britain, who in 197 left the frontier undefended during his campaign against Severus. On his defeat the barbarians broke in, finding forts and fortresses virtually empty. This explains the systematic devastation not only on the Wall but as far south as York, involving the deliberate overthrow of walls and gateways, a thing impossible except when fortifications were left defenceless at the mercy of the invaders. To this occasion belongs the first and greatest destruction, whose traces are everywhere visible in the forts, milecastles and turrets of the Wall.

Virius Lupus, the first governor sent by Severus to Britain in 197, was obliged to buy off the tribes from beyond the Wall in exchange for some of the prisoners they had taken. Then repair began of the damage done to forts throughout the North and to the Wall, where work was in progress in A.D. 205-208. The work was so extensive that Severus came to be described as the actual builder of the Wall; and the reputation was deserved to this extent, that in many places his engineers did in fact reconstruct it from the very foundations.

The punitive campaign was delayed until 208, when Severus came to Britain with his sons, Caracalla and Geta. In 209, all being ready, he advanced against the Caledonians. The campaigns lasted three seasons, with more success than historians admit. The third, however, was preceded by the death of the old Emperor at York in February, 211, and after it Caracalla and Geta (Caracalla became co-Emperor in 198, Geta in 209) arranged peace with the northern tribes and returned to Rome.

Accounts of these Caledonian wars are written to give an impression of failure, but it seems that their main object was achieved. After a short re-occupation of Scotland, Caracalla had re-established Hadrian's frontier, and taught the northern tribes so sharp a lesson that the frontier had peace for nearly a century. Rebuilding in forts along the line of the Wall went on for some time, for inscriptions record much work done in the reigns of Elagabalus (218-222) and Severus Alexander (222-235). Beyond the Wall, a new system of outpost-forts was established (see p. 214), by which the principal routes to the north were held with very strong garrisons, and a strip of territory beyond them was subjected to patrols. Relations with the tribes of southern Scotland became increasingly friendly, and their lands were regarded as Roman spheres of influence.

At the end of the third century the peace of the frontier was again disturbed by the troubles within the Empire. Carausius, who had charge of a fleet to repress piracy in the English Channel, revolted and in 287 assumed the sovereignty of Britain, which he retained until 293, when his power was usurped by Allectus. In 296, Constantius Chlorus reconquered Britain and restored it to Rome. But Allectus had drained the Wall of troops, as Albinus had done almost a century earlier, and the barbarians had broken in. History now records for the first time the group of tribes beyond the Tay known as the Picts. These were the enemies who, from a safe distance, watched continually for an opportunity to plunder the province and smash its defences. After their invasion Constantius had to rebuild the Wall and its forts, not so completely as had Severus, but on a large scale. He was at York, after a punitive campaign in the furthest north, when he died in 306.

Once more the reorganisation of the frontier-defences gave Britain a period of peace and prosperity. The fourth century, despite disturbances beyond the Wall in 343 and 360, was quiet until the great disaster of 367, under Valentinian I and Valens, when a combination of barbarian invaders, from overseas and the far north, set upon Britain from all sides at once. Fortifications were overwhelmed and armies annihilated; of the two commanders-in-chief, the Count of the Saxon Shore fell in battle and the Duke of the British Provinces was rendered immobile, amid widespread devastation.

The situation was retrieved by Count Theodosius, who in

369 came over to Britain with powerful forces, cleared out the invaders, and restored fortifications. Relations with the Lowland tribes were still so friendly that the outpost forts beyond the Wall, reduced in number after 343, could now be abandoned. But this restoration opened the last and shortest phase in the history of the Wall. In 383, Magnus Maximus led the army of Britain in revolt against Gratian and crossing to the Continent, drained the island of its forces. The remains found on the Wall go down to the year 383; after that they become a mere trickle, betokening the presence of either a skeleton force or farmer-soldiers left without pay and dependent upon local resources only. This is more easily comprehensible when it is understood that subsequent order in the district was maintained by the frontier tribes of the Lowlands, who had become allies of Rome and stable political powers. The work of the Wall was done.

III ANCIENT SOURCES

The Notitia

This early fifth-century document, entitled *Notitia Digni-tatum et Administrationum, tam civilium quam militarium, in partibus Orientis et Occidentis,* records the distribution of Imperial officials, civil and military, throughout the Roman world. It embodies earlier material and the list concerning the Wall (*Item per lineam Valli*) is of the early fourth century, in the command of the *Dux Britanniarum*. It is here translated, and the modern names are added in brackets.

Tribune, fourth cohort of Lingones, SEGEDUNUM (*Wallsend*).
Tribune, first cohort of Cornovii, PONS AELIUS (*Newcastle*).
Prefect, first *ala* of Astures, CONDERCUM (*Benwell*).
Tribune, first cohort of Frisiavones, VINDOVALA (*Rudchester*).
Prefect, *ala* Sabiniana, ONNUM (*Haltonchesters*).
Prefect, second *ala* of Astures, CILURNUM (*Chesters*).
Tribune, first cohort of Batavi, BROCOLITIA (*Carrawburgh*).
Tribune, first cohort of Tungri, BERCOVICIUM (*Housesteads*).
Tribune, fourth cohort of Galli, VINDOLANDA (*Chesterholm*).
Tribune, second cohort of Astures, AESICA (*Great Chesters*).
Tribune, second cohort of Dalmatae, MAGNA (*Carvoran*).
Tribune, Hadrian's Own first Cohort of Daci, CAMBOGLANNA
(*Birdoswald*).
Prefect, *ala Petriana*, PETRIANA (*Stanwix*).
Prefect, Aurelius's Own Mauri, ABALLABA (*Burgh-by-Sands*).
Tribune, second cohort of Lingones, CONGAVATA (*Drumburgh*).
Tribune, first cohort of Hispani, UXELLODUNUM (*Castlesteads*).
Tribune, second cohort of Thraces, GABROSENTUM (*Burrow Walls*).
Tribune, first cohort of Hadrian's Own Marines, TUNNOCELUM
(*Moresby*).
Tribune, first cohort of Morini, GLANNIBANTA (*Ravenglass*).
Tribune, third cohort of Nervii, ALIONIS (? *Watercrook*).
Cavalry formation (*cuneus*) of Sarmatae, BREMETENNACUM
(*Ribchester*).
Prefect, Maximian's Own first *ala*, OLENACUM (? *Old Carlisle*).
Tribune, sixth cohort of Nervii, VIROSIDUM (*Bainbridge*).

The great value of the list, as Horsley first perceived, is that it supplies the ancient names of fifteen out of the sixteen Wall-forts, from Wallsend to Drumburgh. It may be repeated that for the Wall the garrison described is that of A.D. 297-367, and this, as inscriptions show, was substantially that of the third century. The remaining eleven names, not in geographical order, need not be considered here; they belong to forts of the hinterland.

The Antonine Itinerary

This is a fourth-century edition of an early third-century road-book, describing the post-roads of the Empire, with names and distances. The Wall is mentioned because two roads cross its line: on the east, from the outpost fort of High Rochester, through the Wall at Portgate to Corbridge and the south (later known as Dere Street); on the west, from the Wall at Carlisle and southward by Cumberland and Westmorland. The *Itinerary* therefore gives the ancient names of Carlisle, Corbridge and other places near the Wall, which it calls *limes* or *vallum*.

The Rudge Cup, Amiens Skillet and Ravenna List

A small enamelled cup found at Rudge in Wiltshire is now at Alnwick Castle. It formed part of a set of ornamental table-ware. Its decoration is a frieze comprising the Wall and its turrets, crowned by the inscription A MAIS ABALLAVA UXEL(L)OD(UN)UM CAMBOGLAN(NI)S BANNA. These names are taken from an Itinerary of the Wall-forts from west to east, including Bewcastle, which is BANNA. A comparable vessel, found in 1949 at Amiens, carries the words MAIS ABALLAVA VXEL(L)ODUNUM CAMBOGLA(NI)S BANNA ESICA.

The Ravenna List is a sixth-century copy of a road-map, of which the British section is derived from second-century sources. It gives the Wall-forts from east to west, including those on the Rudge Cup and Amiens skillet.

IV THE ARMY AND ITS OFFICERS

The Roman Imperial army was divided into legions and the auxiliaries. The legions, each about 5,000 strong, were composed exclusively of Roman citizens, highly-trained and heavy-armed infantry, with a small cavalry detachment. The length of service was sixteen to twenty years with possibility of re-enlistment. The commander was a *legatus legionis* of praetorian rank, holding his commission direct from the Emperor or commander-in-chief of the Army. The second-in-command was the *praefectus castrorum;* the administrative officers were six tribunes, the first of senatorial class, the other five of the wealthy equestrian class, who were given this experience of army organisation as a start to a public career. But the backbone of the legion was the sixty centurions, each commanding a century (*centuria*) of 80 men; and upon them fell the day-to-day maintenance of discipline and efficiency. Each centurion had under him an *optio* or understudy, a *signifer* or standard-bearer, and so forth. There was in fact an elaborate system of subordinates, forming a highly-specialised administrative, clerical and engineering staff.

The legion lived and acted as a unit, having its permanent quarters in a fortress situated some distance behind the actual frontier line; it fought, on the occasion of a campaign, either alone or brigaded with other legions and auxiliary regiments, as a mobile striking force ready to invade enemy territory or to counter-attack against an invader. In Britain, from Hadrian's time onwards, there were three legions; the Second *Augusta* at Caerleon-on-Usk, the Twentieth *Valeria Victrix* at Chester, and the Sixth *Victrix* at York. The last-named was nearest to the Wall.

The auxiliaries differed from the legionaries in many ways. They were not recruited from Roman citizens, but conscripted from among the non-Roman tribes of frontier provinces. Instead of the heavy armour of the legionary, they generally carried lighter equipment, often including their own old-established weapons: thus, the Hamians of Carvoran used their Syrian bow, the Dacians of Birdoswald their traditional curved sword. They were grouped as cohorts of infantry or *alae* of cavalry, nominally either by 1,000 strong (milliary) or 500 strong (quingenary). A cohort, which might be part-mounted (*equitata*), was divided into 10 or 6 *centuriae* commanded by centurions; an *ala* into 24 or 16 *turmae* commanded by decurions; the milliary cohort was commanded by a tribune; the quingenary cohorts and all cavalry by a prefect. Here again there was an elaborate system of subordinates, though less so than in the legion. Length of service was twenty-five years.

Each cohort or *ala* lived and fought as a unit, stationed on the frontier and taking the rough-and-tumble of frontier police-work. In campaigning, the auxiliaries were expected to take the first brunt of the fighting and, if possible, to achieve victory unaided by the legions. Their permanent fort resembled a legionary fortress in miniature: generally about three to five acres in extent and containing within its ramparts barrack-buildings, quarters for the commanding officer, storehouses and administrative offices. All this was thoroughly stereotyped, and scores of forts were built to more or less similar pattern.

Two other formations may be mentioned. A *vexillatio* was a detachment seconded for some special purpose from the ranks of one or more legions or auxiliary regiments; perhaps to campaign forcements, often to undertake building. A *numerus* or " unit " was often levied from newly-conquered districts outside the Empire, was sometimes at least commanded by officers of its own people, and used wholly un-Romanised equipment. The *numeri* may be roughly described as native infantry " units "; their cavalry counterparts were known as *cunei* or " formations ".

V HEIGHT ABOVE SEA-LEVEL OF PRINCIPAL POINTS ON THE WALL

These are taken from Ordnance maps of Northumberland and Cumberland.

	Feet		Feet
Wallsend	95	Winshields	1,230
Newcastle Keep ...	94	Greatchesters ...	690
Newcastle Bridge ...	23	Mucklebank Crag ...	860
Benwell	415	Carvoran	700
Chapel House ...	371	Willowford Bridge ...	360
Rudchester	449	Birdoswald	515
Harlow Hill	495	Pike Hill	541
Down Hill	666	Hare Hill	427
Halton	610	King Water	140
Milecastle 23 (Stanley)	860	Walton	248
St. Oswald's	745	Castlesteads	177
Chesters	240	Newtown of Irthington	223
Limestone Corner ...	823	Stanwix	110
Carrawburgh ...	785	River Eden	35
Sewingshields Crags...	1,068	Beaumont	75
Housesteads	850	Burgh-by-Sands ...	65
Hotbank Crags ...	1,074	Drumburgh	70
Cat Stairs	900	Bowness-on-Solway ...	54

CHAPTER II

A GENERAL ACCOUNT OF THE WORKS

THE Roman Wall is a great fortification, intended not only to act as a fence against northern raiders, but as a corral against which to round them up or a base from which to intercept them. Every fort and milecastle along its course was provided with a gate opening towards the north; while in the land to north there are outpost forts situated on forward roads and garrisoned by Roman troops for centuries.

This great work consists of four chief parts.

    i A Stone Wall and deep, wide ditch on its north side.

    ii Forts, Milecastles and Turrets, to house the garrison.

    iii A boundary Earthwork, now known as the Vallum, south of the Wall and its posts.

    iv Roads for communication and for carriage of stores.

All the works proceed from one side of the island to the other, in more or less direct line and close association. The Wall and Vallum are generally sixty to eighty yards apart. Only near Birdoswald have they been shown to impinge on one another. On the high ground of the central region, however, the Wall seeks the crest of the escarpment of the Whin Sill while the Vallum runs on the lower ground at its tail, thus avoiding the rock. Again, west of Carlisle, on the cliffs of the Eden or the Solway shore, the Wall seizes the positions with best northward outlook. The Vallum, which is neither itself a work of defence nor sited on ground chosen for defensive qualities, runs everywhere in long straight sectors. The Wall extends for eighty Roman miles from Wallsend on Tyne to Bowness on Solway, a distance of about seventy-three and

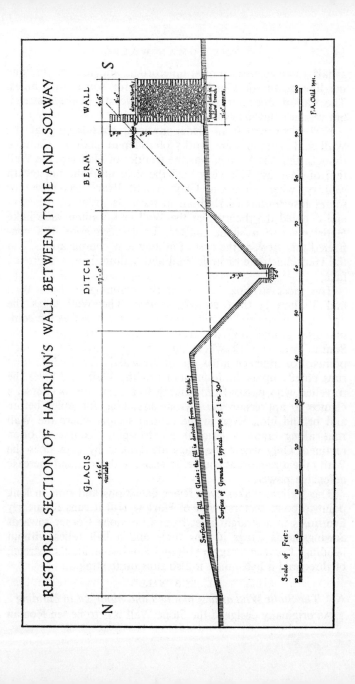

RESTORED SECTION OF HADRIAN'S WALL BETWEEN TYNE AND SOLWAY

N   S

GLACIS   DITCH   BERM   WALL
59'.6"   27'.0"   20'.0"   9'.6"
variable

Surface of fill of Glacis; the fill is derived from the Ditch.

Surface of Ground at typical slope of 1 in 30.

Scale of Feet:
10 0   10   20   30   40   50   60   70   80   90   100

F.A.Child 1941.

a half English miles. Forts, milefortlets and towers continue
the line down the Cumberland coast for some forty miles.
The Vallum does not begin before Newcastle at the east end,
but reaches Bowness on the west.

Earlier writers, from Bede onwards, considered that the
Wall and Vallum were works of different periods. Camden
thought that the Vallum was the frontier of Hadrian, the Wall
that of Severus. This view held the field until the nineteenth
century, when Hodgson, Clayton and Bruce recognised or
found inscriptions of Hadrian in the milecastles of the Wall
and evolved the theory that the Wall and Vallum were alike
Hadrian's and a single scheme. Later excavation has confirmed this view, at the cost of adding new complications, and
the Hadrianic date of both Wall and Vallum is now a proved
fact.

The most striking feature in the planning of both Wall
and Vallum is their straight course. The Wall takes the
dominant position. Shooting across country, it seizes the commanding ground and the crests on the northern line of the
South Tyne and elsewhere and changes direction on high
points. For nineteen miles out of Newcastle the Carlisle road
runs chiefly upon the foundations of the Wall, and gives the
traveller, who passes from summit to summit on its course, a
chance to appreciate the lay-out stretching for miles before
and behind him. Even in the central sector, where the Wall
runs along crags, a straight point-to-point course is often
retained. Only where the crags are broken by gaps does the
Wall take a re-entrant course, to ease the descent and increase
defensive power.

The Vallum makes even fewer deviations and runs in long
point-to-point sectors; west of Harlow Hill it runs for nearly
five miles in a straight line; from Limestone Corner towards
Sewingshields Crags it runs three and a half miles without
bending; between Craggle Hill and Sandysike, another stretch
of three and a half miles, it also runs quite straight.

I   THE WALL

A.   *The Stone Wall as first planned and modified in building*

As originally designed the Stone Wall was to be ten Roman

feet wide, built with coursed ashlar faces, set in mortar, and a rubble core, set in mortar or puddled clay. Foundations to carry a Wall of this width were laid from Newcastle to the river Irthing, a distance of 45 Roman miles. The superstructure, begun from the east, had almost reached the North Tyne when it was abruptly decided to complete the work to a narrower gauge of eight Roman feet, to deepen the foundations and always to set the core in lime mortar. The reason for this was probably economy in labour. At the same time the Wall was extended from Newcastle to Wallsend. This results in the following sequence:

(a) From Wallsend to Newcastle the Wall is *narrow*.

(b) From Newcastle to a point west of milecastle 27 the Wall is *broad*.

(c) From about milecastle 27 to Willowford, the Wall is *narrow,* but stands on the foundation prepared for the *broad* Wall. In this sector, however, the milecastles and turrets, so far as is known, and the original east tower of Willowford Bridge, had been built before the change of plan; and the wing-walls which project from each side of them, ready to bond with the running work when it was built, are *broad*.

B. *The Turf Wall, and its subsequent replacement in stone*

West of the Irthing, the first version of the work was a Turf Wall twenty feet thick at the base and built of cut turves laid in courses. The reason for this choice of material is to be found in local geology. West of the Irthing, limestone ceases at the Red Rock Fault, near milecastle 54. Lime for the grouting of the Wall could therefore no longer be prepared at hand, but the change in material was made for convenience of organisation at the river Irthing. The milecastles of the Turf Wall were built in turf and timber: the turrets were of stone.

Replacement began quickly, and for a stretch of some five miles west of the Irthing, the Turf Wall was soon replaced by the *narrow* Stone Wall on the same line. But between milecastles 49 (Harrow's Scar) and 51 (Wall Bowers) the Stone Wall took a course further north. Here, and here alone, Turf

Wall and Stone Wall can be studied in isolation, and here
their relationship was determined in 1931-35. From west of

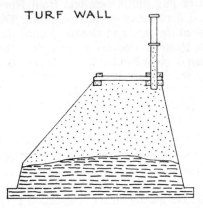

TURF WALL

BUILT IN COURSED TURVES, 18 × 12 × 6 INS. CUBE

0   5   10   15   20   FEET

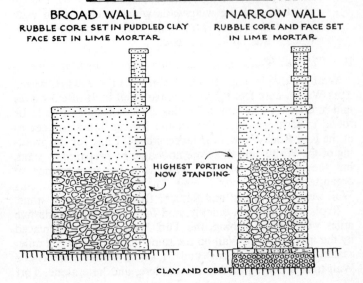

BROAD WALL
RUBBLE CORE SET IN PUDDLED CLAY
FACE SET IN LIME MORTAR

NARROW WALL
RUBBLE CORE AND FACE SET
IN LIME MORTAR

HIGHEST PORTION
NOW STANDING

CLAY AND COBBLE

milecastle 54 to Bowness, however, replacement was deferred, and the Stone Wall, as eventually supplied, was built to an *intermediate* gauge of nine Roman feet. This change took place not later than A.D. 163, but its exact date is unknown. Each replacement incorporated the stone turrets of the Turf Wall and supplied new stone milecastles.

C. *The Height of the Stone and Turf Walls*

In no part of its course is the Wall standing to full height. Bede, whose home was the monastery of Jarrow, almost opposite Wallsend, is the earliest author (A.D. 731) to give dimensions. He describes the Wall, probably as he saw it in his own neighbourhood, as " eight feet wide, and twelve high, in a straight line from east to west, as is clear to beholders to this day " (*Hist. Eccl.* i, 12).

Subsequent writers give the height as greater. Christopher Ridley, curate of Haltwhistle, wrote, about 1572, " The bredth iij yardis, the hyght remaneth in sum placis yet vij yardis ". An anonymous writer, on information from Archdeacon Threlkeld in 1574, observed " Hadrians Wall, begyning abowt a town called Bonus " (Bowness) . . . " and there yet standing of the heyth of 16 fote, for almost a quarter of a myle together ". Camden, who visited the Wall in 1599, says, in Holland's version of the 1607 edition, " there remaineth as yet some of it to be seene fifteen foot high and nine foot thicke "; but it is possible that Camden has misread " xi " as " xv ". These statements leave an impression that Bede's figure, if meant to apply to the original height of the Wall, is too low. Recent inquiries have suggested fifteen feet as the original height of the rampart-walk, to which must be added a parapet and merlons about six feet high, making an effective height of just over twenty feet in all.

The Turf Wall, whose turrets have no ladder platforms (see p. 23) and presumably therefore did not need them, was probably about twelve feet high to rampart-walk.

D. *The Ditch*

Throughout its length, the Wall was protected on the north by a ditch, except where cliffs or the sea rendered this unnecessary. The flat space, or berm, between them is normally 20 feet wide, but in association with the Turf Wall is six feet wide, except in bad ground.

East of Heddon-on-the-Wall the rock-cut ditch, in weathered condition, is 34 feet wide and nearly 9 feet deep; at Stanley, rock-cut, it is 26 feet wide and 11 feet deep; as it descends from Carvoran to Thirlwall it is 40 feet wide and 10 feet deep. At Haltonchesters east gate it was $29\frac{1}{2}$ feet wide and not less than 8 feet deep; at Chesters 27 feet wide and 9 feet deep. At Birdoswald it had a width of 27 feet and a depth of 9 feet. To judge from the sections preserved in virtually original condition because soon filled, at Halton-chesters, Chesters and Birdoswald, it was a standard Roman military ditch, V-shaped in section, with a small square drain-age-channel running along the bottom. Weathering, re-digging and difficult ground can, however, produce wide variation.

The upcast from the ditch is thrown out to the north to form a broad mound or glacis, which heightens the outer slope or counterscarp of the ditch and is made to slope off very gently northwards, so as to afford no cover to an enemy. In some places, however, as at Wall Fell and Appletree, the mound remains unfinished and the upcast lies in tumbled heaps as first dumped in baskets from the digging of the ditch. Nor is the ditch itself always completed. At Cockmount Hill it is dug only to half depth, while further west, at Allolee, it is not dug at all, though its absence is not warranted by the character of the terrain. Again, at the top of Limestone Bank, enormous blocks of whinstone lie as if just lifted out, and a huge mass, as yet unremoved from the middle of the ditch, still exhibits the wedge-holes prepared to split it; after that, the ditch towards the east has not been dug at all. It is suggested that these works were left unfinished at the end of a season's work, when the troops were called off for the winter.

E.   *The Date of Building*

The date of the Wall has been the subject of much con-troversy in the past, but there is no room for controversy now. The Broad Wall from Newcastle to the Irthing, and the Turf

Wall thence to Bowness, were built under the governor Aulus
Platorius Nepos from 122 to about 126, immediately following
Hadrian's visit to the province. The Narrow Wall followed
late in his governorship or under his successor.

II   MILECASTLES, TURRETS AND FORTS

While the Wall was structurally a substantial barrier, it
could not be used efficiently without a garrison to patrol it
and to intercept raiders or to repel attackers. The structures
built to house this garrison form the second part of the fortification and comprise forts, milecastles and turrets.

The idea of placing on the line of the barrier itself both a
fighting garrison in forts and a patrolling garrison in milecastles and turrets was not Hadrian's original scheme. Only
the milecastles and turrets form an integral part of the Wall
as first built: excavation has proved the forts of the fighting
garrison to be secondary to the Wall wherever it has been
possible to test the relationship. The first plan, then, was to
supply the Wall with a patrol garrison only. But it is also
proved that the decision to move the forts forward and to
place them on the Wall itself was a change of plan made while
the work of building the Wall was still in progress: and it
was in no sense the modification of a completed scheme. The
evidence for the sequence is as follows. The original intention, to have only turrets and milecastles on the Wall, is
demonstrated by the fact that at Chesters, Housesteads and
Birdoswald the Wall and a turret have been obliterated to
make way for the fort; while at Haltonchesters, Chesters
and Birdoswald the ditch of the Wall has been filled up for
the same reason. On the other hand, the fact that the forts
came soon is demonstrated at the main west gate of Haltonchesters, which bestrides the filled-in ditih of the Wall but
has also yielded a building-inscription of Aulus Platorius
Nepos, the governor who had built the milecastles and turrets.

A. *Milecastles*

From the very first, then, milecastles existed to house the
troups patrolling the Wall. Their name is derived from their

regular spacing at one Roman mile, now 1,620 yards, from
each other. They were quadrangular fortlets, normally varying from 50 to 60 feet in breadth and from 57 to 75 feet in
length internally. They were built so that the Wall lined up
with their north front; but while the foundations of the Wall

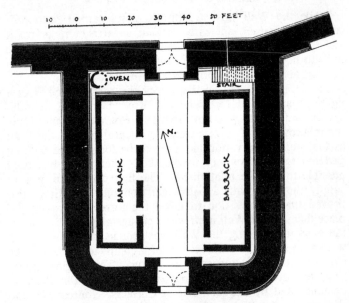

PLAN OF MILECASTLE 48 (POLTROSS BURN).

and milecastle were usually laid simultaneously, the milecastles were normally erected first and supplied with wing-
walls ready to bond with the Wall when its superstructure
was built. The milecastles have wide gateways of massive
masonry in the centre of their north and south walls. Their
south angles are turned in a curve on the outside. Their
internal buildings consist at most of two small barracks, flanking the road between the north and south gates; their rooms
comprise sets of two, living-room and kit-store respectively,
and there are four such sets at most, accommodating 32 men,

but often no more than one set only. Again, while the general design of milecastles is uniform, there are differences in detail.

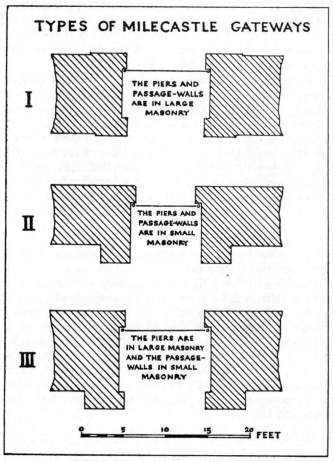

TYPES OF MILECASTLE GATEWAYS

I   THE PIERS AND PASSAGE-WALLS ARE IN LARGE MASONRY

II   THE PIERS AND PASSAGE-WALLS ARE IN SMALL MASONRY

III THE PIERS ARE IN LARGE MASONRY AND THE PASSAGE-WALLS IN SMALL MASONRY

0   5   10   15   20 FEET

Some have their long axis from north to south, others from east to west. There are also three types of gate, as shown on the accompanying illustration. While the differences in size and gate-types are connected with gang-work, those in

garrison-strength are probably connected with the decision
to put the forts on the Wall itself.

On the Turf Wall, milecastles were built to the same design
as those in stone, with ramparts of turf and gateways and
internal buildings of timber. Milecastle 50 TW (High House)
has been completely excavated and remains of others have
been found at milecastles 49, 53, 54, 72 and 79.

Two points may be added on the later history of milecastles. In the Severan period milecastle-gateways were
normally reduced to posterns or foot-passages by narrowing
their width. This is due not to increasing pressure of enemy
attack but to the fact that a broad zone of interception had
now been established (p. 214) far in front of the Wall. This
zone was heavily garrisoned and patrolled, thus rendering
milecastles obsolete as sally-ports on a front-line frontier. But
it has also been discovered that, before this Severan modification, the original milecastle gateways had been supplied with
new pivot-blocks in which to turn their doors and that this
provision, unlike the Severan alterations, is not associated
with the rebuilding of the milecastles after disaster. This can
only mean that during the second century the doors of the
milecastles were for a time systematically dismantled, to be
replaced later in the century. This dismantling, which shows
that for a while the milecastles were disused and left open to
passage unsupervised by any garrison, corresponds to an
obliteration of the Vallum by the crossing system (described
below, p. 30) and to the re-occupation of Scotland in
A.D. 140, when the frontier was moved northwards to the
Antonine Wall between Forth and Clyde. The refitting of the
doors represents in turn a precaution following the disturbance
of A.D. 155-158.

B. *Turrets*

Two turrets, regularly spaced at an average distance of
about 540 yards, occur between each pair of milecastles. They
measure 14 feet square internally and 20 feet square
externally, and can best be understood as the ordinary stone
signalling-towers of the second century, built as an integral

part of the Wall. On the Stone Wall they were built first, as were milecastles, and provided with wing-walls for bonding: on the Turf Wall they were built as square towers without wing-walls, and the turfwork of the Wall was then

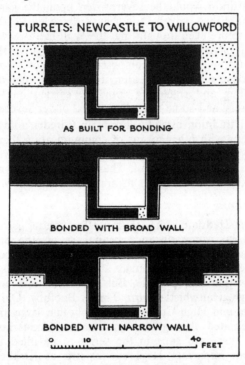

TURRETS RELATED TO THE STONE WALL.

brought up to their east and west sides. They had an upper storey above the parapet-walk of the Wall, which was reached by an internal ladder. This ladder could be drawn up out of reach, and its feet rested upon a little platform, or landing, in one corner of the original Stone Wall turrets.

It is evident that the work of patrolling the Wall, of sending signals along its line and of sending out relays of men to do duty in the adjacent turrets, was the duty of detachments quartered in the milecastles. To discharge this task, a minimum of 1,300 men would be required. The forts, as first designed behind the Wall, could not have met this need; while the drain would be severe even upon the garrison as finally established, which cannot have exceeded 12,000 in all. It has therefore been thought that the Wall had two garrisons, a fighting garrison of cohorts and *alae,* lodged in the forts, and a patrolling garrison composed of units of other kinds, lodged in the milecastles. Later, it was found that the work of patrolling and signalling could be carried on by using fewer turrets, and some were dismantled under Severus.

A local tradition already current in Camden's day credits the Romans with other means of communication than visible signals: speaking-trumpets or pipes, it was fancied, ran along the whole length of the Wall. There is no evidence whatever for such devices. Such pipes as are known are for water.

C. *The Forts*

The first Hadrianic forts to house the fighting garrison for the Wall lay some distance behind it, on the Stanegate, Agricola's road from Corbridge to Carlisle. They occupy or use earlier forts on that road at Corbridge, Chesterholm, Nether Denton and Carlisle. But new forts were erected at Newbrough, Haltwhistle Burn, Throp, Boothby, Old Church Brampton, and High Crosby. It is likely that large and small forts alternated throughout, as between Chesterholm and Carlisle. There are gaps in the series to be filled. West of Carlisle an important large site existed at Kirkbride, but east of Corbridge nothing is yet known of the initial arrangement.

It was next determined to move the fighting garrison on to the Wall itself and, when Platorius Nepos set about building the new forts, the older series was largely demolished. The new forts were of one design and type. They projected beyond the line of the Wall, so that their main north, east and west gates lay north of the barrier, permitting the garrison to deploy very rapidly in order to intercept raiders or to repel attack. These forts are Benwell, Rudchester, Halton, Chesters, Birdoswald (Turf Wall period) and Burgh-by-Sands; and forts in the same series which do not project are Housesteads, Stanwix and Bowness; the last three overlook cliffs or a steep slope, and there should be added Castlesteads, detached behind the Wall on a high cliff.

Yet another series of forts, contemporary with the Narrow Wall, represents a quick revision of the arrangement just described, in the light of experience. These are Wallsend, watching the lower reaches of the Tyne; Greatchesters, surveying the Caw Gap, built in or after 128; and Drumburgh, watching a subsidiary Solway ford. While Carrawburgh, on the west rim of North Tynedale, was built before 133, and the prefect who built Carvoran, in the Tipalt gap, set up an inscription in A.D. 136.

Finally, there are the outpost forts, of which little is known in the second century except their existence in the West, where the outlook of the Wall is limited. These lay at Bewcastle, north of Birdoswald, Netherby in Eskdale and Birrens beyond the Solway. All are known to be Hadrianic, and their later development is discussed below (p. 214).

Three points of importance for the history of the Wall emerge from these facts. First, the initial intention was to equip the Wall itself with a patrolling garrison only, the forts for the fighting garrison being set well behind the patrolled line, as on Hadrian's frontier in Germany. Secondly, the decision to place the fighting garrison on the barrier itself implies that considerable opposition to the new frontier was developing. Thirdly, the third series of forts, filling in awkward gaps in the defence, and the outpost forts, giving warning of impending attack, mean that this opposition had become a stern and frequent reality. Tactically, however, the arrangement of the forts shows that the fighting garrison was not intended to man the Wall and to fight from it, but to go out into the open beyond it and, if possible, roll up the attackers against the barrier which they were attempting to cross. In this fashion of fighting, the extra sally-ports provided by the milecastle gateways were invaluable as the means of developing unexpected converging movements, prepared all unseen behind the cover of the Wall itself.

The forts are planned as rectangles with rounded corners. They are defended by a stone wall, about five feet thick, with

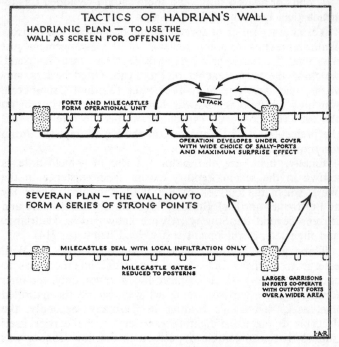

TACTICS OF HADRIAN'S WALL

HADRIANIC PLAN — TO USE THE WALL AS SCREEN FOR OFFENSIVE

FORTS AND MILECASTLES FORM OPERATIONAL UNIT

ATTACK

OPERATION DEVELOPES UNDER COVER WITH WIDE CHOICE OF SALLY-PORTS AND MAXIMUM SURPRISE EFFECT

SEVERAN PLAN — THE WALL NOW TO FORM A SERIES OF STRONG POINTS

MILECASTLES DEAL WITH LOCAL INFILTRATION ONLY

MILECASTLE GATES-REDUCED TO POSTERNS

LARGER GARRISONS IN FORTS CO-OPERATE WITH OUTPOST FORTS OVER A WIDER AREA

I·A·R

THE TACTICAL USE OF HADRIAN'S WALL.

an earth rampart piled against its back, the earth being derived from a defensive ditch or ditches outside the Wall. The gateways are at least four, and always six if the fort projects beyond the Wall. Their portals are often partly walled up, a practice once regarded as a symptom of declining morale in the Wall garrison. But in several cases it is clear that the masonry of the gates was quite new when they were blocked up, and the step is to be connected with the reduction of the Wall-garrison in A.D. 140, when Scotland was re-occupied.

The main street from the front gate of the fort joins the principal cross-street at right angles near the centre of the fort. On its axis and behind the cross-street stood the head-quarters (*principia*). This building was planned with fore-court surrounded by colonnades, giving access to a large covered hall for administration. At the back of the hall lay a series of offices, of which the central one was the regimental chapel containing the standards and dedicated to the worship of the Emperor or his Discipline. In some forts the chapel later contained the entrance to an underground strong-room for pay-chests and regimental savings.

To one side of this central building stood the commandant's house (*praetorium*), ranged in Italian style about a courtyard and often supplied with a private suite of baths. To the other side were granaries (*horrea*), massive buttressed buildings with raised and ventilated, cool and damp-proof floors and fire-proof roofs. These held the grain supply for the year, of which the annual replenishment was a tax in kind upon the province which the Wall defended.

In front of, and behind, the central edifices were rows of long narrow buildings, mostly barracks for the men, but including stables, storehouses or workshops. Each barrack-building housed a century (*centuria*) of 80 men and its centurion; in a cavalry unit each block housed two *turmae* of 32 men apiece and each with a decurion. The men, whether infantry or cavalry, were grouped in mess-units (*contubernia*) of eight each in their own room for living and sleeping, with an ante-room for kit.

These internal buildings can best be seen at Chesters (*principia, praetorium,* barracks) and Housesteads (*principia, praetorium, horrea,* barracks).

A village (*vicus*), established with permission by veterans, camp followers and traders, grew up outside most forts. Excellent examples of its shops and taverns are seen at Housesteads. But the most elaborate external building was the regimental bath-house, of which a fine example is at

Chesters. Essentially it comprised of a suite of rooms graded in temperature from cold to hot; the bather began cold, went gradually from warm rooms to hot room, where he sweated profusely and bathed, and so back to a final cold douche, to close the pores and prevent a chill.

In selecting a site for a fort regard was had to a good supply of water. The springs, rivulets, wells and aqueducts are often known, as at Benwell, Haltonchesters, Chesters, Chesterholm and Greatchesters. At Housesteads, where the main source of supply has not yet been discovered, there is a very large number of collecting tanks supplied from roofs or surface drains.

When the Wall was abandoned, the forts and their villages ceased to be inhabited. Their names, once household words, were soon forgotten. The evidence of the *Notitia*, however, fixes the names of fifteen, though the manuscripts do not always transmit the correct spelling: for example, VINDOLANA should be VINDOLANDA; AMBOGLANNA should be CAMBO-GLANNA; and BORCOVICIUM is for BERCOVICIUM, the late-Roman spelling of VERCOVICIUM.

III   THE VALLUM

The essential part of the Vallum is its ditch, normally 20 feet wide and 10 feet deep, with a flat bottom 8 feet wide, and thus in section quite unlike the Roman military V-shaped ditch. Great care was taken by its constructors to prevent the ditch from falling in or becoming obliterated at points of special engineering difficulty. Where it crossed a steep ravine its sides were revetted with stone, and where it crossed a marsh they were embanked like a canal; or in sandy soil, as at Cawfields, its sides are artificially built in turfwork, capped with clay and resting upon stone flagging. Unlike the ditch of the Wall, the Vallum ditch is never omitted.

The upcast from this ditch is normally piled in two continuous mounds, set 30 feet back from the ditch on either side of it. To make them stand sharply the mounds, 20 feet wide, are revetted with kerbs of turfwork. This gives the

standard original section of the Vallum—mound, berm,
ditch, berm, mound—the whole 120 feet across, the Roman
surveyor's unit known as the *actus*. There is, however, often
a third mound, on one or other lip of the ditch, known as
the marginal mound; this is usually much later in date and is
the product of cleaning out the re-cut ditch.

The Vallum is laid out in truly Roman fashion, running
straight from point to point like a Roman road. Unlike the
Wall, it is not placed upon ground with good outlook or
defensibility, and may run at the foot of a slope equally
useless for defence and for view. It normally runs close
behind the Wall, so that when it approaches a fort attached
to the Wall it usually deviates from the straight course and

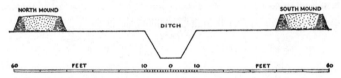

CROSS-SECTION OF THE VALLUM AS ORIGINALLY DESIGNED.

passes round the fort on the south. The approach-road to
the fort from the south was carried across the ditch as
described below. It is not usually so close to milecastles as
to compel any deviation and still less does it impinge upon
the Wall itself. But in the Birdoswald sector it avoids the
Turf-Wall milecastle at High House (50 TW) by a regularly-
planned re-entrant, while to east of that milecastle the north
mound is omitted, as being too near the Turf Wall (see p. 23).
This sector of the Turf Wall was, however, very soon replaced
by a Stone Wall on a course further north. Thus, the Vallum
is shown to be later than, yet virtually contemporary with,
the Turf Wall.

The discovery, in 1935, of the relation between Wall and
Vallum made their relative date a matter no longer of theory
but of fact. The Vallum falls into place as a rearward
boundary strip demarcated by mounds and bisected by a
deep, wide ditch which was an obstacle to all. At the forts,

the causeways across the ditch were blocked at mid-point
by a great unfortified gateway, opened and controlled from
the fort to north, and corresponding to original revetted
gaps in north and south mounds. At milecastles, narrower
causeways, also gated, of which we have only ruined remains (they were later dismantled), crossed the ditch. These,
however, were not intended for public use, for there was no
gap in the south mound by which the public could reach
them. On the contrary, they were for the milecastle's garrison, which reached them through a gap in the north mound

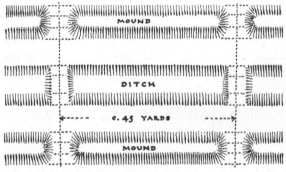

THE OBLITERATION OF THE VALLUM BY CROSSINGS.

and crossed to a patrol-track, of varying solidity according
to the nature of the ground, running along the berm between
the south mound and ditch of the Vallum. Thus, while causeways at forts controlled public roads, those at milecastles
were used solely by patrols from the Wall to intercept tres-
passers upon the military zone. The Vallum thus functions as
a non-military boundary policed by military patrols, a de-
marcation as opposed to a defence. It is the southern
boundary of the military zone.

The original causeways at forts and milecastles are totally
different from the so-called " crossings ". These are gaps dug
through the Vallum mounds, the earth from the gaps being
used to create causeways across the ditch. They are normally made at regular intervals of 45 yards, but in a few

places have been begun but not finished, and very occasionally have not even been begun. Thirty-five of them go to
each Roman mile. This systematic obliteration happened
when the work had not been in use for long, and is both
dated and explained by the reoccupation of Scotland in
A.D. 140.

Subsequently, the Vallum was recommissioned by remov-
ing the causeways and recutting the ditch; the gaps in the
mounds, however, were not filled up again, and can still be
seen at many points, as at Matfen Piers, or west of Carrawburgh or east of Cawfields.

Later still, the re-cut ditch was cleaned out and the
material was piled on its lip, forming a third mound known
as the " marginal mound ". At Limestone Bank, however, the
cleaning out was early, probably following frost action upon
the new rock-cut ditch. This phase in the upkeep of the work
still needs much study.

IV   THE MILITARY ROADS

For lateral communication, the Wall had at first its own
parapet-walk and the patrol-track of the Vallum or the open,
trackless zone between them. Supplies reached the forts by
branch-roads from Stanegate. This road, south of both Wall
and Vallum, gave direct communication between east and
west. It ran from Corbridge to the North Tyne and then by
Newbrough and Chesterholm to Carvoran and Nether
Denton. It appears again at Irthington running to High
Crosby east of Stanwix and at various points in between.
A feature of its western course is the engineering of deep
cuttings in the face of natural obstacles. At four sites along
this road, Corbridge, Chesterholm, Nether Denton and Carlisle, forts of the late first century A.D. have been identified,
showing that the Stanegate began as one of Agricola's roads,
constructed and after his campaigns in northern Britain of
A.D. 79-84. Under Hadrian it must have continued both
eastwards and westwards behind the Wall and its works:
but nothing certain is known of its course, and little as yet
of its goal.

A through road from fort to fort along the Wall was thus not the first element in the scheme. The Military Way, as this road is usually called, came later; not, in fact, until after the obliteration of the Vallum; for it is known in places to ride on top of the north mound of the Vallum at points where gaps had been cut for the crossings. The actual date of construction is not certain, but it may well be Severan, for the earliest dated milestones are of A.D. 213. The structure is that normal for Roman roads. It is some twenty feet wide. Its surface is cambered, the centre being a foot or eighteen inches above the edges. As a rule, it was metalled with small stone, chiefly trap, surfaced with fine gravel, resting upon a heavy bottoming of large stones and edged with kerbs of large stones; but in some places, to bind it better, it had an axial rib of big stones as well as kerbs. Along the slope of a hill, the downhill side was made up by unusually large kerbstones.

For convenience, the Military Way went from milecastle to milecastle, and so from fort to fort, sending off a branch path to each turret. It did not always keep quite close to the Wall, but took the easiest course between the required points. In negotiating the gaps between Sewingshields and Thirlwall, the ingenuity of its engineers has been most successfully applied. While the Wall follows the highest and steepest summits, the road swings along the slope behind it, so as to serve the milecastles by the easiest possible gradients. In most places it is completely grass-grown, but can be distinguished easily by the finer grass which covers it and by the sheep-track that generally runs along it. It is a most instructive example of Roman road engineering.

Finally, in appreciating the design of Hadrian's Wall, it must be recalled that two great lines of communication served the Wall from the legionary bases: one from York, crossing the Wall near Corbridge, with a branch from Binchester to Newcastle; the other from Chester, crossing it near Carlisle, with a branch from Kirkby Thore to Carvoran. The Sixth legion, based at York, would have no difficulty at almost any season in coming to aid the auxiliaries to whom the defence of the Wall was normally entrusted, at whatever point their assistance might be required; and reinforcement could also be had from the Twentieth legion at Chester.

V   QUARRIES AND METHODS OF BUILDING THE WALL

Both faces of the Wall are clad in carefully squared free-stone blocks and the character of these facing-stones is distinctive and tolerably uniform. They measure on the face six or seven inches high by ten or eleven wide and from front to back as much as twenty inches. The face of the stone, exposed to the weather, is cut across the " bait ", or natural bedding of the stone, so as to avoid flaking; while the stone tapers towards the back so as to bond better with the core. The face is normally tooled with a smooth finish, but some-times with distinctive patterns in the form of diagonal cross broaching and diamond broaching, as such tooling is called. The uniformity of their appearance enables anyone, after a little practice, to recognise them at once in the churches, castles, farm-buildings and fences of the district through which the Wall runs. Stones of this size could be most easily wrought in the quarry, most conveniently manhandled and most easily fitted into their bed.

But there are two exceptions. For gates of forts and milecastles, larger stones were used, unless, as at certain milecastles, the steepness of the approach made it difficult to bring up a wagon; for example, 39 (Castle Nick) and 40 (Winshields). Secondly, larger stones are found in the lowest courses of the Wall, but not in its superstructure. They occur in the construction known as Type A, which obtains for seventeen Roman miles westward from Newcastle.

The stone used for the facing-blocks was normally a very carefully selected quartzose grit, which was not only hard but had a rough surface that bonded well with either mortar or clay.

Many of the quarries from which the facing-stones came can be identified. On Fallowfield Fell, not far east of Choller-ford, the face of one of these ancient quarries (see p. 77) was inscribed with the words (P)ETRA FLAVI CARANTINI, " the rock

of Flavius Carantinus ". An old quarry on Barcombe, above
Chesterholm, re-opened in 1837, yielded an arm-purse of
bronze, containing three gold and sixty silver coins, all current under Hadrian. North of Busy Gap wedge-holes still
remain in exposures of rock. Just west of the Stanegate fort
on the Haltwhistle Burn a Roman quarry once bore the

INSCRIBED QUARRY FACE, FALLOWFIELD FELL.
(The stone is now at Chesters Museum.)

inscription, LEG.VI.V; and throughout the central sector
numerous ancient quarries, mostly without doubt Roman,
are visible within half a mile south of the Wall.

In Cumberland, about two miles west of Birdoswald, and
just over a quarter of a mile south of the Wall, Coombe
Crag exhibits many Roman names inscribed by the men at
work. Comparable inscriptions are recorded from Lanerton
and seen at Wetheral, and the most remarkable group of such
records is at the " Written Rock " on the Gelt, near Brampton, where the longest inscription records " a vexillation of
the Second legion, under the *optio* Agricola, in the consulate
of Aper and Maximus ", that is, A.D. 207.

East of the Glebe Farm at Irthington are extensive ancient quarries, while excavations revealed a quarry of consider- able size at Bleatarn. There is another quarry. at Grinsdale, on the river Eden, just north of the Wall, and a famous example once exhibited inscriptions at Shawk, south of Thursby. Generally, however, geological conditions in Cum- berland render quarries both rarer and more distant from the Wall than in Northumberland, so that stone was actually brought across from north of the Solway for use between Carlisle and Bowness.

THE WRITTEN ROCK OF GELT.

Between the ashlar faces, the core of the Wall was packed with rubble, quarried close to the Wall; and the small pit- quarries from which it was taken can frequently be recog- nised. On the Broad Wall, the rubble was set either in mortar or in a mass of tough puddled clay, when only the ashlar faces were set in mortar. The Narrow and Intermediate walls, and all reconstructions, were set wholly in mortar. The principal ingredient of the mortar was lime, also prepared close at hand; for limestone is abundant from Newcastle to the Red Rock Fault, west of the Irthing. An example of the limekilns has been excavated at Housesteads: and the specks of charcoal sometimes found in the lime come from burning in such kilns. The lime was next ground and mixed dry with sand and gravel. Only when this mixture was about to be used, was water added. Mortar thus prepared speedily hardens. In Cumberland, where limestone is scarce, the mortar is less good.

Once the facing-stones were quarried and trimmed and the lime burnt and mixed with sand and gravel, construction could begin. The foundation was laid directly upon bared subsoil, where, below the line to be taken by the faces of the Wall, two rows of flags, from two to four inches thick and from eighteen to twenty broad, were generally set, often in a spread of well-puddled clay. The middle space between the flags was filled with clay and cobbles or broken stone. On this foundation was laid the first course of facing-stones, usually the largest stones used in the structure, occasionally even including a whinstone. The flag-stones of the foundation usually project from one to five inches beyond the first course of facing-stones, and these again usually stand out an inch or two beyond the second course, after which the Wall is taken straight up. Varied treatments of the footings and offsets give a clue to work by different building-gangs. The foundation here described is that of the Broad Wall. The Narrow Wall, in the east, when not laid on the Broad Foundation, had a foundation-trench about 18 inches deep, packed with rubble and clay, upon which the footing-flags were laid. In the west the replacement of the Turf Wall had shallower foundations, whether narrow or intermediate.

When one or two courses of facing-stones had been placed on their beds and carefully pointed, a mass of mortar in fluid state was poured into the interior of the Wall, and stones of any kind or shape that were of a convenient size were " puddled " in amongst it. Whinstones, as being most abundant in the district, were generally used for the filling. Course after course was added, and one mass of grouting imposed upon another, as the work dried, until the Wall reached the required height. When all was finished it formed a solid, compact mass, firm as rock. No scaffolding would be required during erection on so wide a work.

At some points the rubble of the core has been first packed into its place, often laid slanting like herring-bone masonry, and the mortar has been laid upon it with a trowel. In this event the mortar does not penetrate the interstices of the mass and makes a less solid structure. On undulating ground and on some steep slopes the courses of the Wall follow the gentle wave of the surface; but on certain declivities, as at Peel Crag, the stones are laid horizontally, stepping up the hill.

It is clear that the main part of the provincial army was engaged in the task. Inscriptions record the Second, Sixth and Twentieth legions at work on the milecastles, forts and Wall, assisted by men of the fleet and by auxiliary troops. All the masons' work was done by these troops, of whose training it formed part, but they were presumably assisted by native *corvées* for the rougher work, such as clearing, carting or puddling clay or road-making. The original building of the Wall itself was organised by *centuriae*, each building a length of about 45 yards, and seems to have been almost entirely confided to the legions. A facing-stone at each end of the lengths thus constructed was normally inscribed with the name of the century (and sometimes also its cohort) which had done the work. These are the so-called centurial stones, of which over two hundred are known, with up to five recurrences along the length of the Wall. Sometimes, as west of Housesteads, the lengths are shown by slight differences in thickness apparent at the back of the Wall. Stones also mention native communities, but these appear to belong to later reconstruction, carried out by labour-gangs contributed by the tribal units which formed the provincial district government. The Vallum also had centurial slabs, but of these much less is known.

VI THE ORDER OF THE WORKS

It is clear that the building even of the Wall itself was subject to modification. The first plan was to erect a Broad

Stone Wall from Newcastle to Willowford and a Turf Wall from Willowford to Bowness. When the foundation of the Stone Wall had been laid throughout its course the builders began the superstructure. Milecastles and turrets were built first: then the builders of the Stone Wall turned back from the west and began the Wall itself from Willowford almost to milecastle 48, while their companions in the east had built the Wall almost to the North Tyne. At this moment the decision was taken to build forts on the line of the Wall itself, to construct the Vallum behind them (an impossibility until the rearward forts were scrapped) and build the Narrow Wall where the Broad Wall had not yet been erected, and new sectors from Newcastle to Wallsend and from Willowford to west of milecastle 54. All this, together with the adding of yet more forts, constituted close upon ten years' work. The Intermediate Wall, replacing the Turf Wall west of milecastle 54, came later, probably in A.D. 163.

Scale : One inch to one mile

Reproduced from the Ordnance Survey Map with the sanction of the Controller of H.M. Stationery Office

1. WALLSEND—NEWCASTLE GENERAL HOSPITAL

CHAPTER III

LOCAL DESCRIPTION

FORT I   WALLSEND (SEGEDUNUM)

THE municipal borough of Wallsend owes its name to its position, at the eastern terminus of the Roman Wall. Here was planted the fort of SEGEDUNUM, the first listed in the section of the *Notitia* headed *per lineam Valli* and quoted above (p. 7). The site of the fort is good. It commands an angle formed in the Tyne between the Long Reach, extending downstream to the west end of South Shields, and the Bill Reach, which stretches nearly two miles up water. In both directions, therefore, any attempt to slip across the river, then shallower and undredged, could easily be observed by the Roman garrison.

It was not thought necessary to extend the Wall farther along the north bank of the Tyne than Wallsend, but signal-posts may have occupied the south bank as far as South Shields, where there is a 4½-acre fort on the Lawe. This fort was built under Hadrian, and contained in the third century an exceptional number of store-houses for goods brought by sea; for the main sea-going traffic bound for the Tyne kept to the river mouth, as always until the nineteenth century. The fort evidently began as a normal garrison-post and became a supply-base for the Scottish campaigns of 209-11, when the store-houses were built and associated with leaden sealings for bulk goods of Severus and Caracalla. Thereafter the base supplied the Wall. The buildings are displayed in Roman Remains Park, Baring Street, with many relics from the fort in a museum on the spot. At an unknown site near this end of the Wall there was also a large triumphal monument, commemorating the erection of the Wall, and inscribed blocks from it were used for Saxon buildings in Jarrow, where there may well have been another fort, at the mouth of the Don.

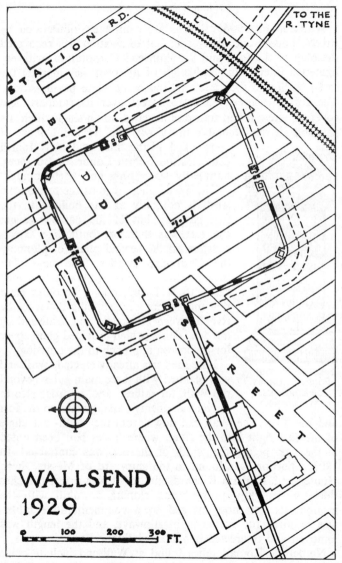

TO THE
R. TYNE

STATION RD.

BUDDLE

STREET

WALLSEND
1929

0   100   200   300 FT.

PLAN OF WALLSEND FORT.

Wallsend fort and its *vicus* are completely obliterated by streets, houses and shipyards; but excavation has recovered the plan of the fort, and the Wallsend Corporation, with enlightened interest in the history of its town, has marked the fort's outline in the streets by means of white paving-stones. The fort measures 453 by 393 feet over its rampart, and covers 4 acres; it had four double gates, and a single ditch. Its garrison in the second century was the Second Cohort of

ALTAR OF THE
FOURTH COHORT
OF LINGONES,
WALLSEND.

Nervii and in the third and early fourth centuries the Fourth Cohort of Lingones, nominally 500 strong and part-mounted.

The Wall, where it joins the fort on the west, is not only of one build with the fort gateway but of the narrow gauge; the fort was therefore built, like Greatchesters, in the second phase of planning the Hadrianic frontier. The new plan included the whole of the Wall from Newcastle to Wallsend; and it becomes clear that marauders were slipping down to the river between Newcastle and Wallsend by the deep denes, which provided good cover for an unseen approach to the crossing.

Like the forts already erected, Wallsend was planned with three main gates beyond the Wall, for sallies: and, in order also to prevent an enemy passing between the fort and the Tyne, the Wall ran down from the south-east angle of the fort right into the river, where traces had been noted in the past before the width of the bed was contracted. In 1903 a portion was found in the ship-yard of Messrs. Swan Hunter and Wigham Richardson Ltd. It was 6 feet 6 inches thick, horizontally coursed and sloping downhill with the ground. Its site, now marked by a commemorative tablet, was required for extension of slipways, and the length was removed and re-erected in Wallsend Public Park.

Numerous Roman relics found at Wallsend include coins going down to Gratian (A.D. 383). In a cellar under the dining-room of Wallsend House, near Horsley's Cousin's House, a well was found. Inscribed stones include an altar dedicated by the Lingones to Jupiter, now in the Museum of Antiquities at Newcastle University; and there is a collection of local antiquities at Wallsend Town Hall. The settlement or *vicus* extended along the north bank of the river. The bath-house seems to have lain south-west of the fort, near the old Fawdon staith, and Lingard describes a structure like a potter's kiln.

FROM WALLSEND TO NEWCASTLE

The Wall started westwards from the south jamb of the fort's west gate. It was the Narrow Wall some 7 feet 6 inches thick, on a foundation 8 feet wide, and is marked as a path in the east enclosure of Carville Methodist Chapel. Owing to tipping of rubbish nothing of the ditch can now be seen east of the Walkerville housing estate. In digging the founda- tions of " The Grange ", just south of the south-west corner of Swan Hunter and Wigham Richardson's recreation-ground, the remains of the Wall were encountered, with a square struc- ture which the workmen called " a cellar ". This was thought to have been a turret, but was in fact probably the north gate of milecastle 1 (The Grange). Early in the nineteenth century the Wall in this vicinity still stood between three and four feet high, covered with brushwood. This whole district, how- ever, was developed for housing in 1939. The new Fossway, which connects Wallsend with Byker Hill, converges with the line of the Wall and passes obliquely on to it, near the pre- sumed site of turret 1*b*. West of Sutton Street this same road occupies the site of the Wall ditch and has obliterated all trace of the Roman works up to the west end of Newcastle.

Milecastle 2 (Walker) was placed by Horsley half a mile east of the summit of Byker Hill, towards which the Wall was aiming, though long since destroyed by quarrying. In 1725, the Wall was here standing in good order, as appears from the " View of the Tract of the Picts' Wall, Newcastleward, from Byker Mill Hill, 4 Septr., 1725 " which Stukeley gives in his *Iter Boreale:* and it must have remained so until 1800, when the *Monthly Magazine* noted that " the foundation of the Roman Wall was taken up at Byker Hill, for the purpose of repairing the highways ".

From Byker Hill the Wall bent slightly to the north and ran down to the Ouseburn on a line parallel to Shields Road, which occupies the site of the berm and ditch. Milecastle 3 (Ouseburn) stood at the east end of Byker Bridge, at the north end of Stephen Street, where a small altar was found and where Bruce noted two of its massive gate-way-stones. Hence the Wall ran down into the ravine and up the other side, but its course is not exactly determined until it passes under the south end of St. Dominic's Church, to run thence almost straight to the Sallyport Gate; after which it begins to turn northward in a gentle curve, passing through the north end of All Saints' Church to the presumed site of mile-castle 4 (Pilgrim Street), on the Tyne Bridge approach,

ALTAR FROM MILECASTLE 3
(OUSEBURN), NEWCASTLE.

where Roman pottery has been found. Where last identified, just west of this point, the Wall was aiming a little north of St. Nicholas's Cathedral; but it seems then to have turned southwards and is said to have been found at Amen Corner, just south of the Cathedral, perhaps there joining the east side of the fort.

The milecastles between Newcastle and Wallsend are abnormally spaced. Normally, milecastles are set with very fair regularity at the distance of one Roman mile (1,620 yards) apart; but here the first two intervals are each some 1,827 yards. Milecastle 1, however, is only some 800 yards west of

Wallsend fort and about 1,200 yards from the terminal point of the Wall in the river. Whether this is related to a further extension of mile-fortlets on the south bank of the Tyne towards Jarrow and South Shields remains unknown. There is no doubt that, since the Wallsend-Newcastle sector is built to the Narrow gauge, not only Wallsend fort but the Wall itself from Newcastle to Wallsend were additions to the original scheme.

FORT II   NEWCASTLE UPON TYNE (PONS AELIUS)

It is clear from the *Notitia* that a fort called PONS AELIUS stood at Newcastle, with the function of guarding the bridge-head, but its outline remains unknown. In 1929, trenches dug immediately south and west of the Castle Keep revealed Roman buildings, one with a hypocaust added after its original construction and still showing the sills of doors and windows. But whether the building lay inside or outside the fort is obscure, and the site may have extended northwards to the Cathedral. The cemetery, to judge by Roman burials, found near Clavering Place, lay west of the fort, while the mouth of the Lort Burn could have been used as a harbour by river craft.

In the early fourth-century, the garrison of the fort was the First cohort of Cornovii, the British tribe whose capital was Wroxeter on Severn. This is one of the rare cases of an auxiliary unit serving in its own province, though most alien regiments brought to Britain or any other province came to have more and more local recruits.

PONS AELIUS took its name from the bridge which Hadrian, whose family name was Aelius, built over the Tyne, on the site of the present Swing Bridge. The Roman bridge seems to have served, with renovations, until a new bridge was built about 1248. This bridge, destroyed by the great flood of 1771, stood on the piers of the Roman Bridge, as did its successor of 1775. When the Swing Bridge was built, in 1866-75, the wooden piles and framework of the foundations of one of the Roman piers were carefully observed and recorded during removal. Both in 1775 and 1875 Roman coins were found, and many coins, thrown from the bridge as votive offerings to the river-god, came from near its site during subsequent dredging. It is known, then, that the Roman bridge had stone piers, each founded on a raft set on massive iron-shod oak piles, with cutwaters up and down stream. The roadway was about 18 feet wide and, to judge by analogy, rested on segmental arches of timber. Twin altars, dedicated respectively

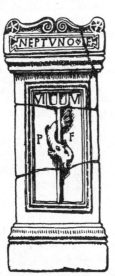 

ALTARS FROM A SHRINE ON HADRIAN'S TYNE BRIDGE (NEWCASTLE).

to Oceanus and Neptune and dredged from the river in 1875 and 1903, came from a bridge-shrine erected by the Sixth Legion and intended to protect the structure against tides and floods. In this shrine, too, reinforcements from the German provinces for the three British legions set up an inscription on their arrival about A.D. 158.

Hadrian's Bridge is important for another reason. Since only the Narrow Wall exists between Wallsend and Newcastle, while the Broad Wall is known in the western Newcastle suburbs and its milecastle sites are exactly spaced _from the bridge, it must be assumed that the Wall was originally planned to begin at *Pons Aelius,* that is, at Hadrian's new river-crossing.

No visitor should leave Newcastle without seeing the very important collection of inscribed and sculptured stones and other material illustrating the Wall and its works, housed in the joint Museum of the University and Society of Antiquaries of Newcastle upon Tyne, situated in the University Quadrangle.

FROM NEWCASTLE TO BENWELL

The Wall west of Newcastle fort is first known at the foot of Westgate Road. Its south face, found within the railings of the Mining Institute in 1951, is marked by a strip of red concrete and an inscribed plaque. The ditch was found both there and, in 1934, just north of the Stephenson monument. From this point almost to Benwell the modern road lies partly north of the ditch and partly over it. No foundations of the Wall have been recovered in this sector, despite careful search; here, however, if the Wall was built to the Broad gauge, it will have had a shallow foundation-course of flagstones only, which could have been completely removed by persons in search of stone. Had it been the Narrow Wall, its deeper foundations of clay and broken stone would have survived, as throughout east Newcastle, since they did not invite stone-robbers.

Milecastle 5 (Quarry House) stood at the junction of Westgate Road and Corporation Street. Its site, where vestiges were seen by Horsley, is exactly one Roman mile from the north abutment of Hadrian's bridge, in the right position for the first milecastle of the Broad Wall, as already explained.

Milecastle 6 must have been at Benwell Grove, but no remains are recorded, nor is any turret known in this sector, so densely covered by modern buildings.

The Wall is now accompanied by the Vallum. Horsley states emphatically that " there is not, in all the space between Cousins House and Newcastle, the least vestige or appearance

of Hadrian's Vallum, or anything belonging to it ". Subsequent research confirms this. The farthest eastward point
at which the Vallum is credibly recorded is close to the site
of milecastle 5, about Elswick Row: and excavations under-
taken in 1929 to discover whether it continued eastward in
the same line, as Bruce and others had supposed, yielded
clear evidence that it did not. What happened to it after
reaching Elswick Row is not certain, but it is highly probable
that it here turned southward and ran down to the river.

The mounds and ditch of the Vallum used to be seen at
the back of the houses on the south side of Westgate Road,
opposite the General Hospital, while to north of the road the
ditch of the Wall was visible, together with the upcast mound
on its north edge. But all has now vanished. The Vallum
ditch can be traced, however, by the subsidences causing
cracks in houses or walls that have been built over its softer
filling. The effect is well seen in Campbell Street, Cromwell
Street, Kingsley Terrace, Ladykirk Road and Condercum
Road, and less well at other points on the course.

FORT III BENWELL (CONDERCUM)

The third fort on the Wall is Benwell, the CONDERCUM of
the Romans, about two miles and a furlong from Newcastle.
It occupies a magnificent natural position, on a level hill-top
about 415 feet above the sea, from which the ground falls
away gently to the north and more steeply on the other sides.
The site was chosen to guard the gap formed by the valley
of Denton Burn, immediately to west. Its northern third now
lies entirely inaccessible below a reservoir. The southern
two-thirds, now covered by the Denhill Park housing estate,
were examined in 1926 and 1937.

The fort measured 581 by 417 feet over its rampart and
covered 5·64 acres. It was garrisoned in the second century
first by cavalry and then by the First cohort of Vangiones
and in the third century by the First *ala* of Astures, mentioned in the *Notitia*.

The north front of the principal buildings is covered by
Westgate Road (A69). Running from east to west, they

comprise the commandant's house, a large headquarters building, twin granaries and a workshop or forge. Little remained of the commandant's house, though hypocausts for heating were observed both in 1751 and 1926, while a well was found in its courtyard in 1959. The headquarters is remarkable for two features. An underground strong-room for pay and savings, located in 1929 to east of the *sacellum*, was cut in the rock, decorated with wall-plaster and lit by a splayed window in its south wall. Secondly, the front court contained a remarkable settling-tank divided into aeration chambers by pierced partitions of strong masonry: this received water from an underground pipe-line, the natural water-table here lying too deep for wells. The granaries were loaded from platforms sheltered by a portico on the *via quintana*, and their dedication-tablet, now in the Museum of Antiquities at Newcastle University, can be translated as " For the Emperor Caesar Trajan Hadrian Augustus, under Aulus Platorius Nepos, Emperor's propraetorian legate, a detachment of British Fleet (erected this building) ". It dates the fort to the governorship of Nepos, which began in 122 and lasted beyond 124. The workshop yielded a mass of forge-sweepings, including local coal, heaped against its east wall.

The road behind these buildings, the *via quintana*, ran between the minor east and west gates, the latter located in 1937. South of it, and east of the axial street, lay a courtyard building, probably a hospital, and another smaller building of uncertain purpose. To west lay two barracks, back to back, accommodating four *turmae* or 128 men in all, one quarter of the garrison. Behind this lay two double stable-buildings and the south rampart, with twin-portalled gateway, angle-towers and single ditch.

Behind the fort the military zone is enclosed by the Vallum, which made an almost regular diversion from the straight course to enclose the site, its ditch being somewhat reduced in width, as a rock-cut section revealed. The causeway across its ditch lay opposite the south gateway of the fort and is seen at the foot of Denhill Park Avenue. It is a natural causeway of undisturbed subsoil, with revetted vertical sides

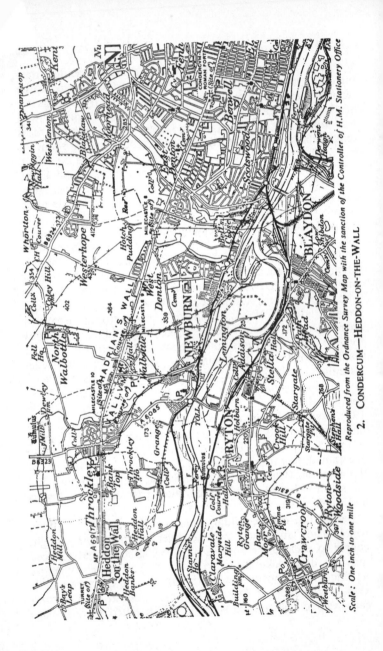

Scale: One inch to one mile

Reproduced from the Ordnance Survey Map with the sanction of the Controller of H.M. Stationery Office

2. CONDERCUM—HEDDON-ON-THE-WALL

of masonry and covered by a heavily metalled road. On the axis of the ditch the causeway was crowned by a monumental gateway, non-defensive in character, with double doors opened from the north, that is, from the fort. In this way access to the military zone from the south was carefully controlled, and the long life of the gateway is attested by

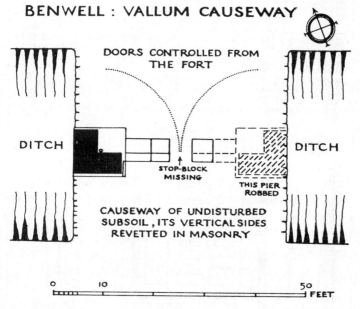

BENWELL : VALLUM CAUSEWAY

DOORS CONTROLLED FROM THE FORT

DITCH

DITCH

STOP-BLOCK MISSING

THIS PIER ROBBED

CAUSEWAY OF UNDISTURBED SUBSOIL, ITS VERTICAL SIDES REVETTED IN MASONRY

0   10   50 FEET

renewal of its pivot-holes in association with a new road-surface. The ditch had very steep sides, as seen in the adjacent sectors, now dug out to full depth. It was drained from the east when the water in it rose too high, by an overflow drain set in the upper part of the causeway. The visitor should on no account miss this Vallum causeway, since it is the only example now seen of the kind with which most forts were once furnished.

The village, or *vicus,* that grew up round the fort lay both north and south of the Vallum and in the later second

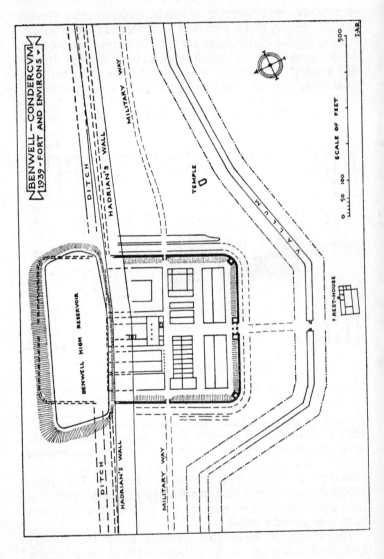

BENWELL—CONDERCVM
1939—FORT AND ENVIRONS

DITCH

HADRIAN'S WALL

MILITARY WAY

TEMPLE

VALLVM

BENWELL HIGH RESERVOIR

DITCH

HADRIAN'S WALL

MILITARY WAY

? REST-HOUSE

SCALE OF FEET

0 50 100 200 500

I.A.R.

century obliterated it. Of its buildings three are notable. The temple of Antenociticus, a deity either local or imported by the Vangiones, is still to be seen in Broomridge Avenue, opening west out of Weidner Road. It is rectangular, 16 feet by 10 feet internally, with an apse at the south end for the stone cult-statue, of which the head, ovoid in shape, with wild hair and Celtic neck-torque, is now in the Museum of Antiquities at Newcastle University. The apse is now flanked

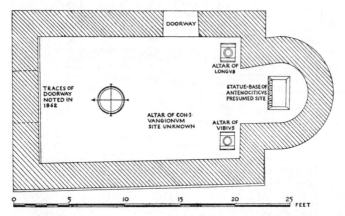

TEMPLE OF ANTENOCITICUS, BROOMRIDGE AVENUE, BENWELL.

by casts of two original altars in the same Museum. One, gracefully carved, is dedicated to Antenociticus and the deities of the emperors, by Aelius Vibius, centurion of the Twentieth Legion. The other has an inscription referring to the promotion of its dedicator, which may be translated " To the god Anociticus, Tineius Longus, given senatorial rank and chosen as quaestor designate while cavalry prefect, by decrees of our best and greatest Emperors, under Ulpius Marcellus, consular!" Anociticus is a blunder in the draft for Antenocitus, and the altar probably belongs to the year A.D. 180.

The second remarkable building was the bath-house of the fort, found some three hundred yards to south-west in 1751, and carefully planned before destruction. It had more than eight rooms, whether original or not, and closely resembles other examples on the Wall of the bath-house which served

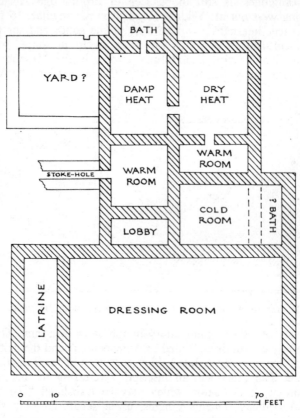

BATH-HOUSE AT BENWELL, 1751.

every auxiliary fort. The visible example at Chesters, described below in detail (p. 92), may best explain its working.

The third structure, not far south of the Vallum causeway, was a large domestic building, closely resembling that overlooking the bridgehead at Corbridge and explicable as a *mansio,* or rest-house for official travellers. Between these buildings of some pretension huddled shops and taverns, the "snake basking beside a warm wall", as Kipling called them. These are not much known in detail: but both excavation and chance finds show that they existed. West of the *vicus,* on Denton Bank, seams of coal once came to the surface, and these have been shown, by analysis of the coal found in the fort workshop, to have been exploited by the Romans. Such open-cast working is not to be confused with the more recent bell-pit workings, on the site of the lower reservoir, which Bruce thought to be of Roman origin.

ALTAR FROM THE
SHRINE OF
ANTENOCITICUS,
BENWELL
(NEWCASTLE).

FROM BENWELL TO RUDCHESTER

The Wall runs across to the south side of the road as it descends Denton Bank and was there found in 1953, in the garden of the Methodist chapel. The site of turret 6*b,* found in 1751, is 308 yards beyond the fort, just east of Two Ball Lonnen, the wide road running north. Milecastle 7 (Benwell Hill) has not been identified. The surface of the road hereabouts was lowered in 1927-28, and the Wall ditch, once visible beside it, no longer appears.

At Denton Burn, to south of the road and east of the stream, occurs the first fragment of the Wall now to be seen above ground. The illustration on the following page was made in the middle of the nineteenth century; and a comparison with the visible remains shows that the structure has suffered little since. In 1927 it was excavated and found to be a typical piece of Broad Wall, 9 feet 1 inch to 9 feet 5 inches thick, laid on a foundation of flagstones and clay. The courses follow the slope, at a gradient of about one in twenty. A little further west, to south of the road, is turret 7*b*, excavated in 1929. It measures 13 feet by 13 feet 9 inches internally, and is recessed 5 feet into the Wall. It showed traces of three occupations, of the periods A.D. 122-196, 205-296, and 297-367. The Wall here is again typical Broad Wall, with very massive stones in the lowest course, many

THE FIRST FRAGMENT OF THE WALL WEST OF NEWCASTLE, AT DENTON BURN AS IN 1848.

weighing over a ton each. Denton Hall itself is a 17th-century building, associated with Lady Mary Wortley Montague, Dr. Johnson and the ghost known as Silky. In the stable a few inscribed and sculptured stones from the Wall are preserved. West of Copperas lane a short length of Wall-foundation is visible on the strip between the two tracks of the Carlisle Road. The southern track occupies the site of milecastle 8 (West Denton), which in 1928 yielded pottery and other relics.

The interval between the seventh and eighth milecastles is probably longer than the normal 1,620 yards, but until milecastle 7 has been precisely located the true state of affairs must remain obscure. It is, however, certain that the western third is widely spaced and that Vallum crossings, once visible to south of Denton Hall, were spaced wider, presumably to retain the standard number of 35 crossings between one milecastle and the next.

The Vallum between Denton Burn and Copperas Lane was destroyed in 1938. Its mounds, boldly kerbed in turf, yielded six inscribed slabs, set into the faces looking on to the berms. This was the first discovery of the fact that the Vallum, like the Wall, had centurial stones. The sector had been built by centuries of the Second Legion and by the first cohort of Dacians, each placing a slab at each end of the length it built. Between the housing estate and St. Vincent's Home the Vallum is still well preserved, with crossings visible. On the site of West Denton School the Vallum ditch was found in 1961 to be rock-cut, almost 11 feet wide across the top and 7 feet 9 inches wide across the flat bottom: it was 12 feet deep with sides standing at 70 degrees. The berms were 35 feet wide and the mounds turf-revetted. Between Wall and Vallum was found the Military Way, 24 feet wide with large stone bottoming.

After passing West Denton, the Wall crossed Sugley Burn, where was once seen a culvert two feet square. Here the Wall and Vallum are about 200 yards apart; they then slowly converge, until at Walbottle Dene they are only sixty yards apart, and thereafter keep nearly parallel until they approach Rudchester. Ascending the hill from West Denton, the road falls into line with the Wall and so continues for $3\frac{1}{4}$ miles, as far as Great Hill. To north of the road, the ditch of the Wall is bold. The Vallum on the south, much ploughed, is relatively faint, but crossings can be detected between Walbottle Primary School and Walbottle Dene, opposite the new County Secondary Schools.

Turrets 8a and 8b have been located in normal position, trisecting the distance between milecastle 8 and milecastle 9 (Chapel House), which lies 300 yards beyond Chapel House Farm, half way down the hill and was excavated in 1929. It measures internally 48 feet 10 inches wide and 60 feet long, and its walls were found to be of the same thickness and construction as the Broad Wall hereabouts. Its north gate, a variant of Type II, was recorded in 1951. This milecastle had been occupied for as long as the Wall was in use and yielded a coin of Valentinian I, while confused fragments of skeletons suggested a violent end. In the next mile, the ditch of the Wall is visible more than once on the north. Turret 9b has been located in Walbottle village, opposite Hawthorn Terrace.

At Walbottle Dene House comes milecastle 10 (Walbottle Dene). Excavated in 1928, it measured 58 by 47 feet internally and its walls matched the Broad Wall. The threshold of its north gateway, with jambs in large masonry, lies at the south-east corner of the front garden. Just before crossing the dene, both Wall and Vallum turn about 20 degrees south, to aim for Great Hill.

The site of turret 10a lies east of Callerton cross-road, in Throckley, and the southward cross-road leads to Newburn, where the Tyne is for the first time fordable. In 1346 David, king of Scotland, crossed this ford on the way to defeat at Neville's Cross, and in 1640 the Scots under General Leslie broke the troops of Charles I at Newburn, causing them to retreat and to leave Newcastle undefended and open to occupation. At the ford there is an ancient framework of stone across the bed of the river. Throckley Bank Top is the computed site of milecastle 11, where no structure or other relics were found in 1928. Near this point a hoard of over 5,000 silvered coins of A.D. 244-275 was found in 1879, just behind the Wall and below the main road. Further west the facing-stones of the Wall were once seen in the road, at a width of 8 feet 6 inches only. Similar reductions occur elsewhere and suggest that the Wall was at some time completely destroyed at such points and rebuilt narrower. Set back from the Royal French Arms public house, on the north of the road, is Frenchmen's Row, originally built for workmen employed in Heddon colliery, but afterwards given to house refugees from the French Revolution of 1789, who erected the dial on the front of the houses. On the south of the road the Vallum is clearly visible.

Turret 11*b* lay beyond Frenchmen's Row, almost on the summit of Great Hill. When the road was remade here in 1926 the Broad Wall was exposed and removed with great difficulty, owing to the hardness of its tough white mortar. On the north of the road, after the houses end, the Wall ditch is seen notably deep. Both it and the Vallum are here cut through fireclay. On the Vallum ditch the tool-marks of the Roman workers are visible and the sides are revetted in masonry where the rock exhibits gaps. The first archaeological sections cut through the Vallum were made here in 1893.

After Great Hill the Wall diverges from the modern road and a length of about 100 yards is preserved in the field to south. The north face stands four courses high and the south face seven; the flag foundation is 10 feet 7 inches wide and the Wall 9 feet 7 inches thick; and the core is still high and thick enough to show that this thickness continued more than five feet above the foundation. At the west end of the stretch a circular structure built into the back of the Wall is not Roman, but a much later kiln. The stones are now all reset in mortar, to preserve the work: when first examined the core was set in tough puddled clay.

The ditch of the Vallum is seen in the hamlet of Heddon-on-the-Wall as a sunk lane parallel with the main road. Mile-castle 12 (Heddon) lay at the west end of Town Farm but has been entirely destroyed. A large hoard of Roman coins in wooden boxes was found here in 1752, but without record. In the beautiful Saxon church, with Norman chancel, an illegible centurial stone occupies a window-sill in the south aisle.

The main road (A69) now turns off to south, to Horsley, Corbridge and Hexham; the minor road (B6318) which occupies the site of the Wall goes straight forward. Its history is as follows. When the Pretender's forces appeared before Carlisle, in 1745, the Royal troops were lying at Newcastle, where the enemy had been expected. At that time no road fit to carry artillery existed between Newcastle and Carlisle, so that General Wade was obliged to abandon Carlisle and to seek his enemy by a more southerly route. After this, the road now known throughout the district as the " Military " or

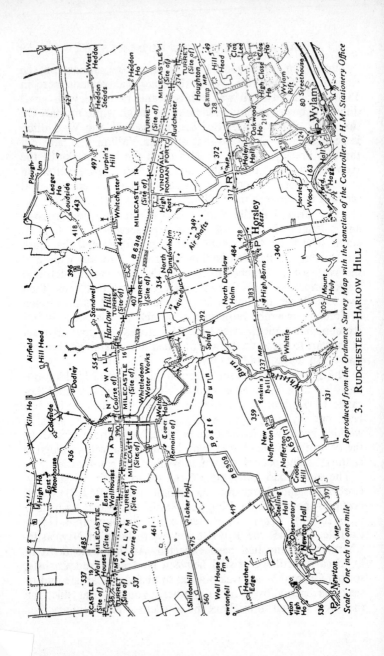

Reproduced from the Ordnance Survey Map with the sanction of the Controller of H.M. Stationery Office

3. RUDCHESTER—HARLOW HILL

Scale : One inch to one mile

the " Carlisle Road " was made. For miles together the tumbled ruins of the Wall were levelled flat to form it, despite the antiquary Stukeley's protest. Formerly the facing-stones were often seen protruding through the macadam, but are now hidden by the bitumenised surface.

From Heddon, the Wall and the Vallum run straight and parallel towards Rudchester. Both ditches are finely preserved. The Wall-ditch, 210 yards east of turret 12b, was found in 1956 to be 27 feet wide by 7 feet deep, with an upcast mound 30 feet wide. Turrets 12a and 12b, in normal positions on the south side of the road, were excavated in 1930, as was milecastle 13, visible as a low platform south of the road, 150 yards beyond Rudchester burn. A hoard of gold and silver coins, the latest dating to A.D. 168, was found here in 1776. The milecastle measures internally 59 feet 9 inches from east to west and 50 feet from north to south; it is thus of short-axis type, while its east and west walls are narrow-gauge, 7 feet 8 inches thick, and its gates are of type I. Turret 13a, also dug in 1930, has walls 4 feet thick, like Nos. 12a and 12b. Beyond this point facing-stones formerly visible in the road proved, as was confirmed in 1930 at milecastle 13, that the Wall hereabouts was the Broad Wall, 9 feet 3 inches thick. The next cross-road lies just outside the east rampart of the fort of Rudchester.

FORT IV RUDCHESTER (VINDOVALA)

Rudchester, the ancient VINDOVALA and the fourth fort on the Wall, lies 6¾ miles from Benwell. It was garrisoned in the fourth century by the First cohort of Frisiavones, rendered in the *Notitia* as *Frixagorum*. It guards the valley of the March Burn to west and an ancient route southwards to the Tyne ford at Newburn. An earlier garrison, of unknown name but commanded by prefects, was presumably cavalry.

The fort measured 515 by 385 feet over its rampart, covering about four acres and a half. To north of the road a platform and slight traces of its ditch mark its position: to south, the west and south ramparts are clearer. The farm-buildings to the south lie beyond them.

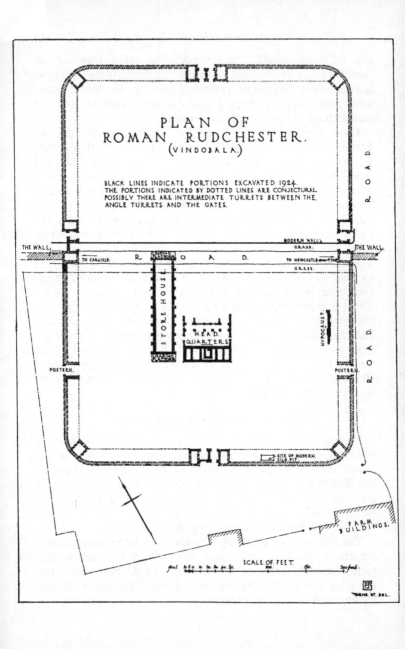

PLAN OF
ROMAN RUDCHESTER.
(VINDOBALA.)

BLACK LINES INDICATE PORTIONS EXCAVATED 1924.
THE PORTIONS INDICATED BY DOTTED LINES ARE CONJECTURAL.
POSSIBLY THERE ARE INTERMEDIATE TURRETS BETWEEN THE.
ANGLE TURRETS AND THE GATES.

ROAD

MODERN WALL.
GRASS.

THE WALL

THE WALL

TO CARLISLE. R O A D. TO NEWCASTLE-ON-TYNE.

GRASS.

STORE HOUSE.

LOADING PLATFORM.

HYPOCAUST

HEAD.
QUARTERS

HEATING APPTS.

POSTERN.

POSTERN.

ROAD

SITE OF MODERN
SILO PIT.

FARM
BUILDINGS.

SCALE OF FEET.

feet 100 80 10 20 30 40 50 100 150 200 feet.

The Wall joined the fort at its main east gate, leaving its forward area projecting to north. As at Haltonchesters, Chesters and Birdoswald, the Wall-ditch already existed before the fort, and Haverfield's excavation of 1902 made contact with the massive foundations laid to carry the main west gate across its line.

Excavations in 1924 were directed to gates and principal buildings. Four gates were of the usual double type and two, at the ends of the *via quintana*, single portals. But the south gate had been reduced to a single opening about the middle of the second century, by converting its west portal into a guard-room and fitting the east portal with inner doors; while the main west gate, as at Haltonchesters, had been totally blocked, so soon after its erection that the threshold remained unworn by traffic. Inside the fort, the headquarters building and its underground strong-room were examined; a granary was identified and a hypocaust in the commandant's house was partly revealed.

ALTAR TO MITHRAS FROM RUDCHESTER (NEWCASTLE).

The Wall at the west gate of the fort had a first course fourteen inches high and above it a cavetto-moulded plinth. This elaborate treatment is not known elsewhere on the Wall. The Vallum makes a slight southward turn some 700 yards east of the axis of the fort and passes it some 240 feet to south; no deviation in its line comparable with that at Benwell was therefore required.

South and south-west of the fort lay the usual village (*vicus*). The sole visible structural relic lies to west of the farm, on the brow of the hill. It is a cistern twelve feet long, four and a half broad and two feet deep, with an outlet hole close to the bottom at one end. When discovered, in 1766, it had a masonry partition across it, and contained many bones and an iron implement, described as like a three-footed candlestick. Its purpose is obscure.

Shrines are also known. About 1760, a life-size statue of Hercules was found and is now at Newcastle. In 1844, five altars to Mithras, the Persian god of light, were discovered, and his temple was excavated in 1953. It had been built during the third century and seems to have lasted into the fourth, when it was deliberately destroyed. The first building was 43 feet long by 22 feet wide, with a segmental apse for a

CENTURIAL STONE AT
RUDCHESTER.

sanctuary, and an irregular vestibule, or *narthex*, attached to its front. It was built on the site of earlier but different structures, destroyed in A.D. 197. Later the *narthex* was demolished and the main chapel received larger benches and wooden pillars supporting its roof. Small altars for offerings and a thurible were ranged along the benches. Five altars, discovered in 1844, had occupied the sanctuary; and one has, carved on its front, a wreath and other symbols which leave no doubt that the unnamed god is Mithras. The inscription means in English: " To the God (Mithras) Lucius Sentius Castus, (centurion) of the Sixth legion, set up this gift ". Of the remaining four altars two are dedicated by prefects, one recording a restoration of the shrine; the fourth is dedicated to the unconquered Sun-god Apollo and the fifth is uninscribed.

Many stones in the old farm-buildings and adjacent fences are Roman. A few fragmentary inscriptions, built up in the walls, include part of a gravestone, with some such text as [D(IS) M(ANIBVS)] AVR(ELI) [. .]RINI [VI]XIT [AN]NIS[. .] At the house are millstones and a centurial stone that reads [CO]H IIII > PEDI QVI, " the century of Pedius Quintus of the fourth cohort ".

FROM RUDCHESTER TO HALTON

Turret 13*b* lay some 80 yards west of the fort. Milecastle 14 (March Burn) is seen as a low platform crowning a slight knoll east of the stream and south of the road. On the south of the road also a former public house, known as " The Iron Sign ", is largely built of Roman stones, and in the front wall are three centurial stones, reading, though not with ease, > .ISI VERI, COH VIII > FL.LATINI and > HOS[IDI]LVPI respectively. Next comes a knoll called Eppies Hill, the Vallum skirting its south side and the Wall seizing its rocky top, upon which Horsley saw remains of turret 14a. The Wall ditch is very distinct to north of the road all the way to Harlow Hill. The Wall and the Vallum on the summit are within thirty yards of each other, but soon draw apart; for while the Wall inclines to the north, aiming for the next high point, the Vallum continues in a straight line.

A little more than half a mile beyond Eppies Hill, mile-castle 15 (Whitchester) is marked by a bold platform and hollows where its walls have been robbed. The Vallum is here 400 yards from the Wall and, after a slight turn, runs quite straight for five miles to Carr Hill. The ditch of the Wall is again in fine order on the forward slope. At Harlow Hill the Wall passed through yards south of the road and milecastle 16 stood here, but, as at Heddon, no trace exists. At the bottom of the hill lie the Whittledean reservoirs of the Newcastle and Gateshead Water Company.

The village of Welton, about half a mile south of the cross-road, contains the ancient pele-tower called Welton Hall, built almost entirely of Roman stones. Over the door the inscription " W.W. 1614 " commemorates Will of Welton, of whose enormous strength strange tales were told. Nearly opposite Welton Hall, and close behind the Wall, was found a Roman milestone of the Military Way, set up by the Emperor Antoninus, known as Caracalla, in A.D. 213.

On ascending the hill, 200 yards beyond the reservoirs, milecastle 17 (Welton) is seen on the south as a bold hump. Excavation in 1931 showed that, like milecastle 13, it had narrow side-walls, 7 feet 11 inches thick, and measured internally 53 feet east and west by 49 feet north and south, with gates of type I. The Vallum converges upon the Wall without deviating from its straight course, until, at a point

300 yards beyond the milecastle, the two almost make contact.

Turrets 17a and 17b, in normal positions, were excavated in 1931. All known turrets east of milecastle 17 have a door in the south-east corner and a ladder-platform in the south-west; in these turrets the positions are reversed. This variation seems to correspond to one in the Wall's construction. Hitherto there has been one course of large stones above the flag foundation and then a single offset, which reduces the Wall to its standard thickness (type A): henceforward, instead of one course of large stones, there are three courses of small stones between foundation and offset (type B). The transition occurs about 190 yards west of milecastle 17.

Milecastle 18 (East Wallhouses) lies about a furlong west of the Robin Hood Inn, where an accommodation-road turns south to a farmhouse. It was found in 1931 to measure 53 feet 8 inches from east to west by 59 feet 6 inches from north to south, and its side walls are 7 feet 9 inches thick. Its gates are of type I.

All the earthworks of the Barrier are here very well preserved. The Wall ditch is in excellent order; while the Vallum shows gaps in its mounds and causeways in its ditch; in other words, complete crossings unremoved by any subsequent cleaning-out of the ditch. These can be seen best immediately east of the southward lane at Wallhouses, and again a quarter of a mile beyond Matfen Piers, where a unique additional feature appears, namely, a small mound like a traverse, obstructing the south approach to each crossing.

Turret 18a, partly excavated in 1931, was exceptionally well preserved and its ladder platform was standing to full height, with six stone steps. The old toll-house partly covers turret 18b, excavated in 1959, when no occupation later than the second century was found. Just beyond it, a road runs south to Corbridge, about four miles away, and Hexham, some three miles further.

Where the piers of the old gateway to Matfen estate mark a by-road to the north, occurs milecastle 19 (Matfen Piers).

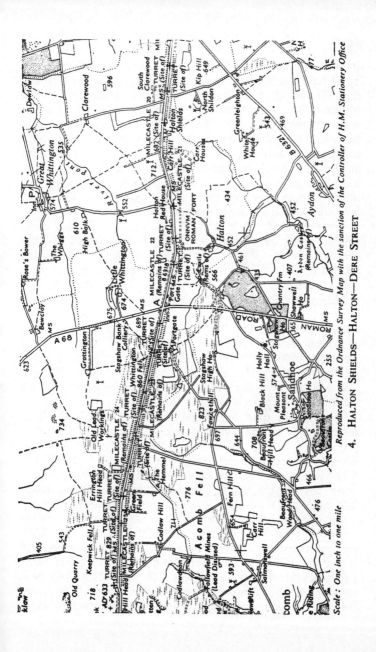

4. HALTON SHIELDS—HALTON—DERE STREET

Scale : One inch to one mile

It measured internally 56 feet 3 inches from north to south by 53 feet 4 inches from east to west. Its gates are of type III. In 1931, an altar dedicating " a shrine, with altar to the Mothers, by a detachment of the first cohort of Vardulli, under the direction of Publius D.V.", was found just outside the south gate of the milecastle, associated with the second-century road surface, and is now in the University museum at Durham. Bruce recorded that facing-stones visible in the road here gave a width of under eight feet for the Wall, but found it over nine feet wide a mile farther on. This must indicate reconstruction, as west of Throckley.

Turret 19*a*, found in normal position in 1932, had been disused under Severus, its walls largely demolished and the recess built up. Turret 19*b* was built largely with clay instead of mortar. The doors of both turrets are in the south-west corner.

Milecastle 20 (Halton Shields) was examined in 1935. It is about 59 feet long and 54 feet 4 inches from east to west, with gates of type III. The Vallum here runs so close to the Wall, that its north mound will have lain only five feet away from the milecastle's south gate, if it was not omitted, as at Harrows Scar and High House milecastles (49 and 50 TW). The Military Way accordingly runs on the north berm of the Vallum and keeps to it as far as Down Hill.

The modern road avoids the summit of Carr Hill, where facing-stones of the Wall, 9 feet 6 inches wide, used to peep through the nineteenth-century surface and a southward bend could be observed. The Wall and Vallum, now fifty-five yards apart, run virtually parallel for some distance, when the Vallum bends sharply south to avoid the rocky hummock of Down Hill. It then returns as sharply to something like its former direction, and the diversion may be compared with that round the marsh at Carvoran. The Wall, on the other hand, runs straight across the hill and its ditch is cut in solid rock. This relationship of Vallum and Wall led Bruce to observe justly that " If the Vallum had been constructed as an independent defence against a northern foe, and nearly a century before the Wall, an elevation which so entirely commands the Vallum would surely not have been left open to the enemy, especially as it would be just as easy to take the Vallum along the north flank of the hill as the south ". But the siting of the Vallum elsewhere, as at Heddon-on-the-Wall, tells with equal decisiveness against Bruce's own explanation of it as a southward defence.

Excavation in 1893 showed that the Vallum mounds had here been revetted in stone instead of turf. Gaps in the mounds are very plain, but the causeways in the ditch have been removed, and there is a marginal mound on its lip.

Down Hill is pitted with hollows, no doubt marking Roman quarries. The modern lime quarry and kiln on its west edge lie close to the site of milecastle 21. West of Halton Red House turret 21a was found in 1935, in normal position, eighty yards east of the fort of Haltonchesters.

FORT V HALTONCHESTERS (ONNUM)

Haltonchesters fort was garrisoned by a cavalry regiment, the *Ala I Pannoniorum Sabiniana,* named after a Sabinus who first raised it and called *Ala Sabiniana* in the *Notitia.* An inscription confirming the *Notitia* and first observed by Camden, is now at Trinity College, Cambridge. It is from a monumental tomb erected to a native of Noricum, who died at 30, by his brother Messorius Magnus, himself a trooper of the *Ala Sabiniana,* on double pay (*duplicarius*).

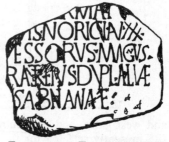

FRAGMENTARY TOMBSTONE FROM HALTONCHESTERS, MENTIONING THE *ala Sabiniana* (TRINITY COLLEGE, CAMBRIDGE).

The fort lies on the east bank of Fence Burn, seven and a half miles west of Rudchester. The site does not make close contact with Dere Street, which passes through the Wall at Portgate, three-quarters of a mile to the west; nor is its northward outlook the best to be had. But a water-supply is assured by an aqueduct from the source of Fence Burn, while the site commands both the deep ravine of that burn to the west and a ridge by which men could steal round the marshy headwaters of the Pont to north.

The Wall, running below the south verge of the Carlisle road, joined the fort at the south towers of its main east

HALTON –HUNNUM, 1936.

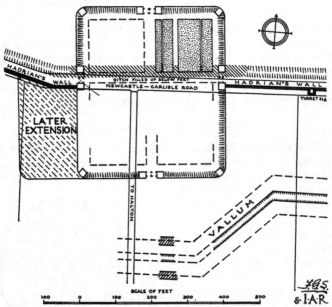

and west gates, and no doubt originally ran through on the site presently selected for the fort, as at Chesters. The ditch also had been already dug before the fort was built and when the fort came, it was filled up to carry the north portal and north tower of both gates and the north half of the main street connecting them. The Vallum, its ditch contracted in size as at Benwell, made a diversion, presumably symmetrical, round the fort but only its east arm has been traced. The planning of the site, however, was complicated

by a westward extension under Severus, which enlarged the
fort on the south side of the Wall only, thus creating a
unique L-shaped plan. The
original fort measured approximately 460 by 410 feet
over the ramparts, the extension gave to the rearward
portion a total width of some
570 feet, the two areas being
4·3 and 4·8 acres respectively.

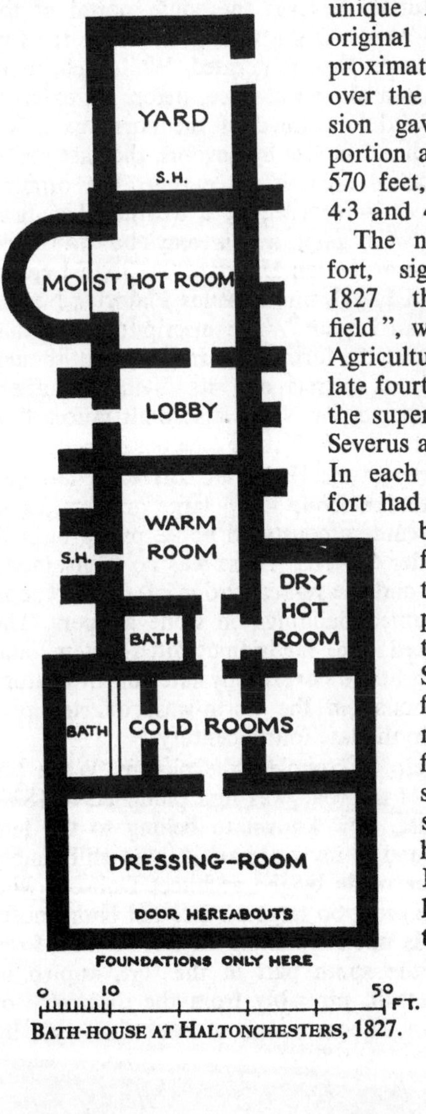

The northern third of the
fort, significantly called in
1827 the " Brunt-ha'penny
field ", was examined in 1936.
Agriculture had removed the
late fourth-century layer: only
the superimposed buildings of
Severus and Hadrian were left.
In each phase, however, the
fort had held cavalry, stables
being here identified
for the first time on
the Wall. The street-
plan had differed in
the two periods: the
Severan fort had been
focused upon a monu-
mental fore-hall, 160
feet   long,   which
spanned the thirty-foot
street in front of the
headquarters building;
Hadrian's   architects
had been less ambi-
tious.   Their   most
massive   masonry,
carrying the main
east and west gates

BATH-HOUSE AT HALTONCHESTERS, 1827.

across the obliterated Wall-ditch, had been hidden from view. These gates had twin portals and towers containing guardchambers, and under Severus the south portal of the east gate had been blocked. At the west gate, where the fort was terraced high above the obliterated Wall-ditch, both portals had been blocked almost at once, before an external road was provided. Little remained of the north gate, but its west portal was reduced in size by Severus, the east portal being presumably blocked then, if not earlier. The original building of the defences is recorded by a weathered dedication-tablet from the west gate, which may be translated " For the Emperor Caesar Trajan Hadrian, the Sixth Legion, Victorious, Dutiful and Loyal, under Aulus Platorius Nepos, Emperor's propraetorian Legate ". The inscription, like that from Benwell, shows that the forts of Hadrian's Wall, though obliterating the Wall, its turrets and its ditch, are afterthoughts in a single scheme, for Nepos also built milecastles, the earliest structures on the Wall itself (see below p. 127).

The southwest quarter of the Hadrianic fort was examined in 1960-61. West of the *principia* lay a large granary, as at Rudchester; and next came a courtyard house partly built in timber and rebuilt under Severus. There was no Constantian occupation of the fort and the re-occupation of A.D. 369 took the form of timber-framed buildings on stone sleepers. The west extension covered the Hadrianic ditch-system and housed a Severan bath-house covered by late fourth century buildings. The bath-house in the north-west quarter presumably also belongs to the late fourth century.

Older discoveries help to complete the picture. When the area of the fort north of the road was first ploughed in 1827, an elaborate bath-house, now known to belong to the late fourth century, was found in its west half. A plan still visible in air-photographs, was made by the architect Dobson, who supplied details to Hodgson. So large an internal bath-house, a rarity on the Wall, is not uncommon in late-Roman forts of the Continent. In the south part of the fort, known in Horsley's day as Silverhill, probably from the discovery of Roman silver coins, an elaborate slab of Antonine style by the Second Legion was found in 1753, and is now at the Museum of Antiquities in Newcastle. Halton Tower and church also embody Roman stones. In the church-yard a Roman altar stands upside down, its inscription obliterated; at the door of the house is a small altar with carved sacrificial dish and jug, and in the garden wall a weathered grave-stone exhibits a traditional funeral-banquet scene. A much defaced male figure in the wall of the back buildings is probably not Roman.

FROM HALTONCHESTERS TO CHESTERS

West of the Fence Burn the road cuts through a prominent hummock, the site of turret 21*b*. On ascending the hill, the platform of milecastle 22 (Portgate) is faintly visible. Excavation in 1930 showed that the side walls were eight feet thick, the north wall having the normal thickness of nine feet three inches; the internal width was fifty-five feet and the north gate, of type III, had been blocked in reconstruction by Severus, doubtless because the adjacent gateway carrying Dere Street through the Wall served more than all purposes of the milecastle gate.

Dere Street, in fact, crosses the Wall at right angles 263 yards ahead. Horsley observed traces of a guard-house or gate, " half within the Wall and half without ", and the ditch indeed appears to turn northwards round such a structure. The road, now the A68, was no doubt made soon after Agricola's advance into Scotland. To south, it links the Wall with York, the legionary headquarters, by way of the forts at Corbridge, Ebchester, Lanchester, Binchester and Catterick. Northwards, it aims for the forts at Risingham and High Rochester. On the moors beyond them, grass-grown and deserted, it exhibits much of its original construction and reaches the Scottish border beyond Chew Green, where there is a fortlet and a very remarkable group of temporary camps.

Going south along A68, in 2¼ miles one arrives at the Roman site of Corbridge, situated on a level terrace, east of the watersmeet of Tyne and Cor Burn, and half a mile west of the modern township. Systematic excavations here from 1906 onwards have shown it to be a military site, first a fort

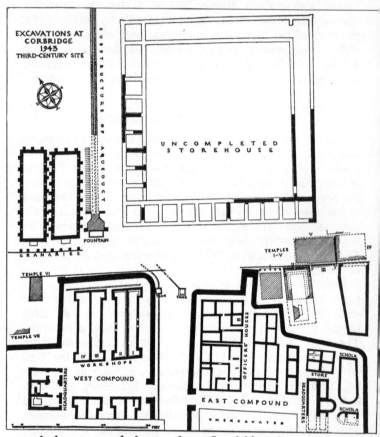

EXCAVATIONS AT
CORBRIDGE
1943
THIRD-CENTURY SITE

SUBSTRUCTURE OF AQUEDUCT

UNCOMPLETED STOREHOUSE

FOUNTAIN

G R A N A R I E S

TEMPLE VI

TANK   TANK

TEMPLES I-V

TEMPLE VII

WORKSHOPS

WEST COMPOUND

HEADQUARTERS

OFFICERS' HOUSES

EAST COMPOUND

UNEXCAVATED

HEADQUARTERS

SCHOLA

STORE

SCHOLA

and then a supply-base, whose flourishing days were connected with the Roman occupations of Scotland; later, in the third and fourth centuries, it became an arsenal, where weapons and other things were manufactured by specialist detachments from the Second and Twentieth legions, and a large civilian settlement grew up round it. The site is now under the Ministry of Public Buildings and Works, and the excavations and museum are an essential part of any visit to the Wall. Corbridge is the point where the Stanegate, aiming for Carlisle left the Roman North Road. It has been traced westwards across the Cor Burn but is not known again until the west bank of the North Tyne. Corbridge Saxon church tower, in which the stones of a Roman arch are used, is notable; and even more so is Hexham Priory, where St. Wilfrid's crypt, of about A.D. 675, is largely built with Roman stones from Corbridge: there is a Severan building-inscription in the roof of the north side-passage of the crypt and the tomb-stone of Flavinus, standard-bearer in the *ala Petriana*, is now in the south transept, while other carved and inscribed stones are seen in the nave, along the north wall.

Returning now to Portgate, the Wall and Vallum, about eighty yards apart, are very well preserved for the next three miles. The Wall Ditch is magnificent; in places the upcast from it lies on its outer margin, in rough and unlevelled heaps, as if the workers were away for the dinner-hour, and in fact attesting unfinished work on the part of the ditch-digging gang.

Turret 22*a* was found in 1930, nearly 200 yards beyond Portgate. Hereabouts the facing-stones of the Wall could once be seen in the road; it was six feet wide, indicating reconstruction, but east of the summit the full width of nine feet six inches was again observed. Turret 22*b* lay 540 yards farther on, where a lane branches to south. Now the Vallum becomes impressive and is seldom in more perfect state. In 1801 old William Hutton wrote with enthusiasm: " I climbed over a stone wall to examine the wonder; measured the whole in every direction; surveyed them with surprise, with delight, was fascinated, and unable to proceed; forgot I was upon a wild common, a stranger, and the evening approaching . . . lost in astonishment, I was not able to move at all ".

Milecastle 23 (Stanley), seen as a low mound to south of the road, was examined in 1930. Its side-walls are 10 feet

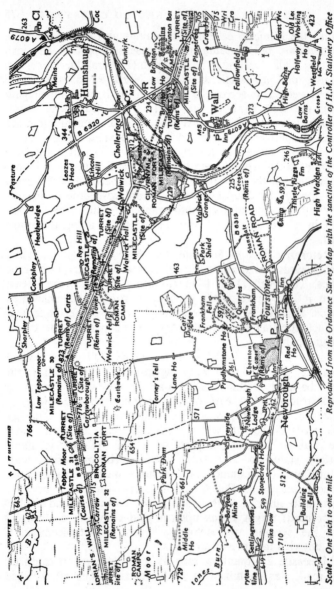

Reproduced from the Ordnance Survey Map with the sanction of the Controller of H.M. Stationery Office

5. BRUNTON BANK—CHOLLERFORD—CHESTERS—CARRAWBURGH

Scale : One inch to one mile

thick, its internal width is fifty feet. There are traces of a ditch round it, as at milecastles 25 and 51. In 1952, the Vallum was also here excavated. Its south mound runs through uninterrupted, but the north mound is broken by a gap giving access to the milecastle. The ditch had been re-cut, and, if an original causeway existed, it had been removed. Turret 23a has been found by the roadside 543 yards beyond the milecastle, and turret 23b, 542 yards farther on again. On the summit the ditch of the Wall, cut in rock, is 26 feet wide and 11 feet deep, while the Wall, ten feet five inches wide, formerly peeped through the road. Looking east from the summit the Vallum is again very striking; the marginal mound is well developed, and the Military Way runs on the top of the north mound, doing this from just west of mile-castle 23 to just east of No. 26, there being little room between Vallum and Wall.

In the north-east corner of the first arable field to south of the road, milecastle 24 (Wall Fell) is a distinct platform and was found in 1930 to be fifty feet wide internally, with side walls 10 feet thick. Two fields farther on, at a dip in the road, is the site of turret 24a; 24b comes opposite the ruined Tithe Barn in a field to south. About a furlong short of the nineteenth milestone, the platform of milecastle 25 (Cod-lawhill) may be recognised to south, opposite a white gate in the north wall of the road. Its dimensions resemble those of milecastle 24, but it was protected by a ditch.

Turret 25a lay a little east of Hill Head, where to right of the easternmost top-floor window of the main farm, a centurial stone is seen, with an inscription of the Eighth Cohort, and century of Caecilius Clemens. About half a mile south of this point, at Fallowfield Fell, a Roman soldier, Flavius Carantinus inscribed his name upon the rock which he was quarrying (see p. 33). But this " written rock " has been cut out and removed to Chesters Museum, to protect it from defacement.

At Hill Head the road swings to south and the Wall now runs through fields, some fifty yards to north. The Vallum also crosses the road, which now occupies its south berm.

North of the Wall is seen St. Oswald's church, which contains a Roman altar used as a cross-base; and at the roadside stands a modern wooden cross, erected to commemorate the original wooden cross set up at battle of Heavenfield, where St. Oswald, king of Northumbria, defeated the British king Cadwallon in 634. Bede states that " The spot is shown to this day, and held in much veneration, where Oswald, being about to engage, erected the standard of the holy cross, and on his knees prayed God to assist his worshippers in their dire need. . . The place is called in English *Heofenfeld,* or Heaven Field . . . it is near the northern Wall by which the Romans formerly enclosed Britain from sea to sea . . .

CENTURIAL STONE AT HILL HEAD.

Hither, also the Brethren of the church of *Hagustald* " (Hexham), " not far away, have made a habit of going once a year, on the day before that on which King Oswald was later slain, to keep a vigil for the salvation of his soul, and, having sung many psalms, to offer for him in the morning the sacrifice of Holy Oblation. And since that good custom has spread, they have lately built and consecrated a church there " (*Eccl. Hist.*, iii, 1-2). The existing church is post-Saxon, but Saxon crosses contemporary with Bede have been found on the site and confirm his statement.

Turret 25*b*, south-west of the church was excavated in 1959, yielding no pottery later than the second century. The Vallum runs straight on, behind a white cottage and through the little farm, to cross the road again and so under the house of Planetrees Farm, where the Wall also crosses the road obliquely. Here is milecastle 26, discovered in 1930, whose dimensions match those of the previous three. A little farther on, to north of the Wall, is Black Pasture Quarry, which yielded the stone used for the Wall in this area. It is first-class, close-grained sandstone, to be cut in blocks of any size.

Opposite the quarry and south of the road, a conspicuous piece of Wall is preserved by the Ministry of Public Building and Works. This is the piece that was saved by the tears of old Hutton, who wrote on 22 July 1801: " At the twentieth milestone. I should have seen a piece of . . . Wall, seven feet and a half high, and two hundred and twenty-four yards long: a sight not to be found in the whole line. But the proprietor, *Henry Tulip,* Esq., is now taking it down, to erect a farm house with the materials. Ninety-five yards are already destroyed, and the stones fit for building removed. Then we come to thirteen yards which are standing, and overgrown on the top with brambles ". According to local tradition " the old man wept " and induced the owner to save this fine piece. As it happens, it preserves the junction between the Broad Wall on the east, and a sector only six feet thick, of the kind seen again at turret 26*b*. The meaning of this variation is obscure.

The road descends steeply, with a fine length of the Wall ditch on its south side. Turret 26*a,* opposite High Brunton House, was examined in 1959 and produced two levels, but nothing later than the second century. The road then swings to north and passes Brunton House, west of which stands another fine piece of Wall. This, however, is reached by a stile on the Hexham-Chollerton road (A6079), about 200 yards south of the cross-roads at the foot of the hill. It is a fine stretch of Broad Wall, still seven feet high, and exhibits nine courses of facing-stones. The faces have been reset in mortar, as found, but the core, now also mortared to preserve it, was originally set in tough puddled clay. In front of the Wall the ditch is very bold. Here is turret 26*b,* excavated by Clayton in 1863, and measuring internally twelve feet nine inches by eleven feet six inches. It has a doorway, with threshold checked for monolithic stone jambs, as at turrets 29*a* and *b.* Its north wall now stands eight feet and a half high, in eleven courses. The wing-walls of the turret are of the Broad gauge, ready to fit the Broad Wall, and that on the west does so, but on the east the Wall is six feet wide only.

The Carlisle road crosses the North Tyne on Chollerford bridge, built in 1775. A medieval bridge, under repair in 1333, now lies some 300 yards downstream and wholly west of the river, on the island formed by the weir at Red Lion cottage. The abutments and piers of a second narrow bridge, seen at low water immediately downstream from the existing bridge, presumably belong to the bridge broken in 1733 and destroyed in 1771 by floods.

From turret 26b the Wall runs straight to the river. Between the Hexham road and the disused railway a low platform indicates milecastle 27 (Low Brunton), excavated in 1952. It is a long-axis milecastle set in the Broad Wall, measuring 58 feet 9 inches by 48 feet internally; its gateway is a variant of type II, found at milecastles 9 and 33. Then follows one of the most remarkable features on the whole Wall, the abutment of the Roman bridge excavated in 1860 by John Clayton. This is reached from the east side of Chollerford Bridge, by a path alongside the disused railway.

The ditches of both Wall and Vallum may be distinguished running down to the river. As it approaches the bridge abutment, the Wall is the narrow Wall, standing on the Broad foundation. It is, however, only six feet four inches thick, but stands up to eight feet eight inches high. It terminates in a tower twenty-two feet square, standing upon the abutment. The main face of the abutment is twenty-two feet long, accommodating a roadway about 20 feet wide, and the two sides are heavily splayed. The south side, originally as long as the north, has also been lengthened to check scour by the river. At the north end of the abutment, five courses of facing-stones stand six feet above the foundation course. Some are very large and come from Black Pasture Quarry, a mile to east. All have a lewis-hole and grooves for iron tie-rods run in with lead. Their distinctive feathered tooling will be noted; and a *phallus*, for good luck, is carved on the southward water-face.

This fine bridge was not the first. Embedded in the abutment is a mass of earlier masonry, forming a water pier. The main mass of a second pier of similar size is incorporated

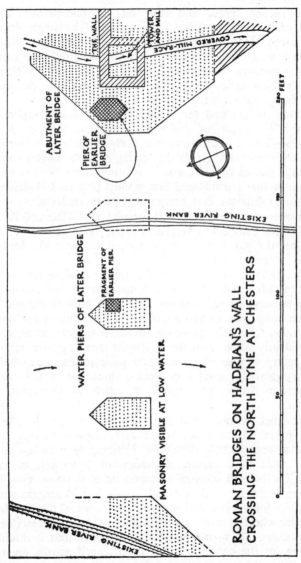

DIAGRAM OF ROMAN BRIDGES AT CHESTERS.

ROMAN BRIDGES ON HADRIAN'S WALL CROSSING THE NORTH TYNE AT CHESTERS

ABUTMENT OF LATER BRIDGE

PIER OF EARLIER BRIDGE

THE WALL

TOWER AND MILL

COVERED MILL-RACE

EXISTING RIVER BANK

WATER PIERS OF LATER BRIDGE

FRAGMENT OF EARLIER PIER

MASONRY VISIBLE AT LOW WATER

EXISTING RIVER BANK

0   50   100   150   200 FEET

in the second larger and later pier in mid-stream. The stones of both these earlier piers were tied by single dove-tail cramps. This indicates an earlier and narrower bridge, designed, as at Willowford, to carry the Wall only, its piers having cutwaters both up and down stream, like Hadrian's bridge at Newcastle, whereas the cutwaters of the second and wider bridge face upstream only.

Clayton, seeing that the second bridge was contemporary with the Wall, ascribed this earlier bridge to the period of Agricola. But at Willowford the bridge which also carried the Wall or its walk across the Irthing exhibits similar small and large phases (p. 160); and its relation to the Wall is such as to show that the enlarged bridge must be a post-Hadrianic alteration, while the first bridge belongs to Hadrian.

Voussoirs built into the first later pier at Chesters show that the first bridge was arched in stone, again as at Willow-ford, but the stone piers of the second bridge undoubtedly carried a timber superstructure. Several of its stones, now scattered about, have grooves for timbers, while no arch-stone of this period has been found among the ruins. A highly unusual stone, however, is a large bollard six and a half feet long and one and a half in diameter; its square base is moulded to match the string course of the abutment, and has evidently come from the abutment face, together with a fragmentary second example. Their purpose may have been to carry gratings, chains or hecks, slung across the river downstream from the bridge, to catch anyone passing below it.

A channel, or race, four feet wide, runs across the abut-ment, passes through the tower and extends beyond the excavated area in both directions. Entering by a built open-ing, it must have served an undershot water-mill in the tower. To the mill belongs a second unusual stone, now in Chesters museum; it is two and a half feet in length, with eight slots for spokes, and it formed the core of the hub for the water-wheel to work a geared mill, of the type described by Vitruvius. Slabs one foot thick, which formed a double covering for the channel, have been snapped across, apparently by the weight of ruins fallen upon them. They were found as they lie, in tumbled disorder partly due to stone-robbing. No legible inscribed stone tells the history of the bridge, but the mill-race was evidently not built until after the second bridge had been extended southwards.

The later bridge had three water piers. It is ascertained by excavation that one lies immediately under the present embankment, west of the abutment. Two others are seen in the river bed when the water is low. They have a single pointed cutwater facing upstream, lewis holes and grooves for tie-rods. The west abutment, of the same type as its fellow, is mostly submerged, but in low quiet water can be seen from the west bank, where a large mass of masonry suggests that it also carried a tower.

East of the river, about a mile and a half northward along the road to Wark at Chollerford church, the monolithic columns on the south side of the nave are Roman and probably come from Chesters, while a Roman altar, once inscribed to Jupiter Optimus Maximus, is inverted for use as a font.

FORT VI   CHESTERS (CILURNUM)

No fort on the Wall so combines accessibility with interest as Chesters, now under guardianship of the Ministry of Public Building and Works. A summer express 'bus service passes it; and, close by, the Bellingham 'bus route from Hexham, which runs all year round, has a stop at the George Hotel.

Chesters is the CILURNUM of the *Notitia* and was garrisoned by the Second *ala* of Asturians, 500 strong. It is a sister fort to Benwell, which was occupied by the First *ala* of the same folk. It is five and a half miles from Halton-chesters, and its purpose was to guard the west side of the bridge across North Tyne, just described. The fort measures 582 by 434 feet over its ramparts and covers five and three-quarter acres. It is planned as the usual rectangle with rounded corners; and forms a prominent grass-grown platform masking the levelled mass of masonry and floor-levels.

The defensive wall is five feet thick, backed by an earth bank and fronted by a ditch. As at Benwell, Rudchester and Haltonchesters, there were six gateways.

As in all the Wall-forts so far described, the Wall leaves about one-third of the fort projecting northwards. The Narrow Wall, standing upon the Broad foundation, abuts on the fort at the south towers of its main east and west gates. But the Wall ditch, already dug before the fort was laid out, runs right across the site presently occupied by the fort, and is buried below the main cross-street, as at Haltonchesters. The foundations of the Broad Wall and of turret 27*a* also underlie the fort, the turret at 136 feet west of the inner face of the east gate. Finally, when the fort ditch was dug, it was brought so close to the foundation of the Broad Wall as to cause it slightly to collapse. The course of the Vallum here is not exactly known, but there are good reasons for thinking that it avoided the fort by the usual symmetrical diversion.

The visitor reaches the fort at the north gate (*porta praetoria*), which had twin arched portals, separated by piers of masonry at back and front; each portal is about 12 feet wide and was closed by double doors turning on iron pivots in socket-stones, still seen behind the front jambs of the entrances. The west portal, once blocked, exhibits an original sill-stone fresh and unworn, showing that the blocking took place early, probably when the Wall itself was abandoned in A.D. 140 in favour of the Antonine Wall. The east portal, kept in use, has sills and a central stop-block of Severan date, the Hadrianic ones buried beneath them. There is also a Severan aqueduct channel, with cover-slabs of re-used stones, feeding the fort from springs to north-west. On either side are guardchambers, with doors opening into the gate portals. Each guardchamber formed the lower storey of a tower.

The north rampart, clearly seen as a mound running east and west, leads on the right to the north-west angle and so to the west rampart and main west gate (*porta principalis sinistra*), again with twin portals and guardchambers. The

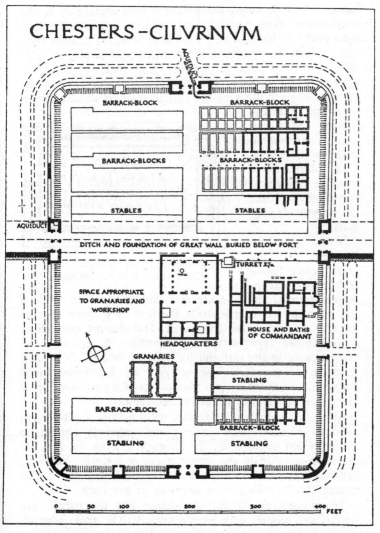

CHESTERS FORT: VISIBLE REMAINS IN BLACK; REMAINS KNOWN
BY EXCAVATION SHADED; REMAINS INFERRED IN SINGLE LINE.

Narrow Wall on broad foundation is seen coming up to the south tower. Both portals of this gate, as at Haltonchesters, were evidently blocked very soon after being built, since their sills are unworn; the north portal has a later paving of large stones; in the south the original iron socket-cups of the pivots are still in place. At both this and the main east gate, the final stage in blocking the portals involved walling up the inner and outer entrances and filling the intervening space with rubble. This formed a massive platform on which to plant the Roman spring-guns.

DEDICATION-SLAB OF AN AQUEDUCT-HEAD, CHESTERS (CHESTERS MUSEUM).

The guard-chamber of the north tower has a feature of exceptional interest. In its north-east corner has been built a settling-tank, fed from outside the fort by a stone channel introduced through the front wall. The channel exemplifies a well-known type of military aqueduct. It enters at the highest point in the fort and its source is one of the springs to north of the fort. The bringing of this water (*aqua adducta*) is recorded by two inscriptions of a governor Ulpius Marcellus, probably of the early third century.

About forty-eight yards further south comes a gate (*porta quintana sinistra*) with single portal, precisely similar to that now left exposed on the opposite side of the fort. At the south-west angle are scanty traces of a tower, followed, half-way between the angle and the south gate, by a fine interval-tower, with central doorway at the back.

The south gate (*porta decumana*) has the usual twin portals and towers with guardchambers. The *spina* separating the two portals is more complete than any other at Chesters. The iron collar which held the pivot of a door in the west portal could once be seen in the pivot-hole and another is now in the Museum. The covered stone channel outside the gate is a branch of the aqueduct described at the west gate, on its way to feed the bath-house.

The gates of Chesters fort are the first at which can still be seen in position the evidence of destruction and repair, of which the forts and milecastles of the Wall afford such abundant proof. It is clear that whenever enemies succeeded in capturing the Wall they had no intention of holding it, but burnt and damaged buildings to the utmost. Excavation shows that these disasters happened in 197, when Albinus, having taken all available troops to Gaul in support of his claim to the Empire, was annihilated by Severus; in 296, when the usurper Allectus, murderer and successor of Carausius, employed most of the provincial garrison in defending himself against Constantius Chlorus; and about 367, when much of Britain was overrun by simultaneous barbarian attacks. The disasters are marked by three superimposed layers of burnt matter and débris regularly found in occupied sites on the Wall: for when the Roman troops rebuilt the forts, they did not remove all the fallen ruins, but, levelling them down, laid new floors, rebuilt partly demolished walls, or built new Walls upon a higher foundation. This is evident in the south gate. When the east guardchamber was excavated three layers of débris were found. In the east portal the flagged floor is raised considerably above that of the west portal on a mass of loose stones; the rear threshold, much worn, is of re-used inverted gutter stones, and the front threshold exhibits later pivot-holes and stop-block for the doors. Here, incidentally, may also be seen the fallen block from the central pier, pierced to receive the upper door pivots. The west portal, on the other hand, exhibits no such change, since it was blocked when still new, the blocking-wall being now removed to reveal the unworn threshold.

In the east guardchamber of this gate was found much of a bronze tablet of A.D. 146, a *diploma* or *tabula honestae missionis,* the recipient's copy of the official decree giving Roman citizenship to an auxiliary soldier on his honourable discharge from twenty-five years' army-service and legalising his marriage, past or future, with any one wife. Clayton presented the original tablet to the British Museum and an exact replica is on view in Chesters Museum.

Beyond the south gate are seen an interval-tower and the south-east angle-tower. The Walls of both stand about twelve courses high, enclosing an area about thirteen feet by ten. Two infant-burials were found in the interval-tower. The external face of the rounded south-east angle stands well-preserved, eight courses high.

Northwards along the east rampart lies the *porta quintana dextra*, a single portal twelve feet wide, which takes the place of an interval-tower and was no doubt surmounted by a tower itself. To this gate came traffic from the bridge and beyond, along the Military Way of which the mound appears.

Next comes the main east gate (*porta principalis dextra*). The guardchambers stand up to twelve courses high. Each portal has been crowned by an arch, both at back and front, and the impost-mould on the south rearward pier remains, with slots on its upper surface to hold the shuttering for the arch. The thresholds of each portal are quite unworn, suggesting they were soon blocked, like the west gate at Halton-chesters. A drain is seen in the flooring of the south portal. The Wall joins the south tower, a little south of the portal.

The headquarters (*principia*) lies in a large railed enclosure in the centre of the fort. Its north half is a courtyard, bordered on three sides by porticoes. Bases of the piers which supported the porticoes remain, and the gutter-stones for their eaves-drips are in position. The court, which contains a fine well, has later been flagged, and on one paving-stone is carved a large *phallus,* a device much used in the Roman world to avert the evil eye.

South of the courtyard a large hall extends across the building. Its monumental central doorway is now largely removed, and there are two lateral openings, probably once filled with grilles for light. Then comes a north aisle, entered from the porticoes and also by side-doors. The west side door was used by small wheeled vehicles, perhaps hand-carts, for bulky

objects. At the west end of the hall are the foundations of a
raised dais (*tribunal*), on which the commandant administered
justice. On the south side lie five rooms. Three have wide open
fronts, once spanned by arches, from which the fallen stones
lie near. The central room, divided into ante-room and shrine,
was the chapel (*sacellum*) in which the regimental standards
were kept; the pair of flanking rooms were offices for regimental records, to west, and for pay, to east.

The pay-room had a large underground strong-room
reached from the *sacellum* by steps, in which a fine building
record of the First cohort of Dalmatae was re-used. An oaken
door, bound and studded with iron, was found at the entrance
of the vault, but fell to pieces shortly after exposure. On the
strong-room floor were a number of plated *denarii*, chiefly
of the reign of Severus, as if it had been added in the reconstruction after A.D. 197. The roof is constructed with three
parallel arched ribs, bridged by large slabs.

Two remarkable sculptures, now in the Museum, probably
once decorated the *principia*. The first is the top of a relief,
depicting a trooper holding a flag (*vexillum*) inscribed in
Latin, meaning " While the Emperors are safe, the Second
ala of Antoninus's Own Asturians is happy! The valour of
the Emperors!" These loyal sentiments belong to A.D. 221-2,
when Severus Alexander became the colleague of Elagabalus,
who is the Antoninus mentioned and later erased in disgrace.
The second piece is a statue of Cybele, standing upon a heifer,
and probably belongs to a group representing Alexander
Severus as Jupiter Dolichenus and Julia Mamaea, the
Empress, as his consort.

Two building-inscriptions in the Museum, from the headquarters and the north east barrack area respectively, are re-
used, but belong to A.D. 139, recording work done at the fort,
pending the Antonine re-occupation of Scotland, by the
Second legion. Two further building-inscriptions, also in the
Museum, have been re-used as paving-stones. The first, inter-
preted by Professor Eric Birley, is from the *principia* of about
A.D. 205, mentioning Severus and his sons, the governor
Alfenus Senecio and the procurator Oclatinius Adventus. The

second belongs to Elagabalus and Alexander Severus, and commemorates the dedication of a building on 30 October A.D. 221. The name of the building is lost, but its provision doubtless helped to inspire the contemporary expression of

NORTH-EAST CORNER OF THE COMMANDANT'S BATH-HOUSE, CHESTERS.

loyalty recorded above. A small fragment of a building-record, set up by the same prefect not earlier than 223, was re-used as building-material in the bath-house.

To east of the *principia* are three blocks of buildings excavated by Clayton in 1843. That immediately adjacent is a long range only nineteen feet wide, of late date and uncertain purpose, overlying earlier structures visible here and there. East of this a rectangular building is much altered by whole-sale insertion of hypocausts, some very roughly built. Some of their furnaces occupied disused passages of the original building. This is probably the commandant's house, increasingly equipped with heating. The easternmost block is certainly the commandant's private bath suite. It is admirably built, with moulded base-course on the external walls, though it was not the first building on the site and the hypocausts are patched with re-used columns. In a ruined part of the north wall was found the fine recumbent statue of Neptune, now in Chesters Museum. A pair of cold baths in one of the northern chambers was once lined with red cement, now weathered off. Immediately to south is the dressing-room; to east an intermediate warm room and a hot room with apse. The ruined walls harbour plants of beauty and some rarity, notably the yellow fumitory (*Corydalis lutea*) and the shining-leaved crane's bill (*Geranium lucidum*); also the rock-plant, *Erinus alpinus,* which, however, was planted after the discovery of the bath-house.

Well to north of these buildings, and also railed, is a street running east and west, with central gutter again lined with numerous re-used shafts of columns. On either side is a long barrack-building, divided into uniform rooms, mostly holding eight men apiece and fronted by a veranda. A group of large rooms at the east end held decurions and other officers. Here some partition-walls are of poorer construction, as though the rooms had been sub-divided at a later date, and at least one room appears to have been a stable, presumably for the decurions' mounts.

The refuse from these blocks affords a clue to the soldiers' diet. The shells of oysters, mussels, cockles and limpets were noted. Romans, and in particular the folk of Roman Spain, relished sea-food and, though Chesters is thirty miles from the coast, its Spanish garrison procured some. Bones of red deer, roebuck, and extinct type of ox, wild boar, and sheep or goat were also frequent. It is clear that the soldiery threw the discarded bones of their food amongst the rushes that covered their floors, and allowed them to stay there. But the fact that bones do not occur in the earliest level, suggests that this unsavoury habit was not always allowed.

Between the barracks and the north rampart lay other

narrow barracks, later rebuilt. They resemble a group just
behind the east end of the south rampart, of which the colonnade is still visible, later insertions having been removed.

Extramural buildings can be detected flanking the Military
Way leading to the bridge, and the Wall has been laid bare

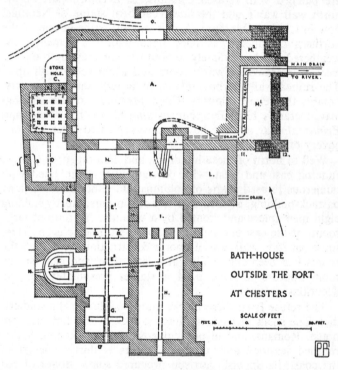

BATH-HOUSE

OUTSIDE THE FORT

AT CHESTERS.

SCALE OF FEET

between the east gate and the river. At the edge of the river,
when the stream is clear, the foundations of the west abutment of the bridge are seen.

Downstream from this abutment, and near the edge of the
river comes the large and imposing regimental bath-house. A
small porch, O, added late, leads into a large dressing-room
(*apodyterium*), A, about forty-five feet long and thirty wide

and paved with flagstones, on which the bases of central pillars to carry the roof were found. Its west wall contains seven round-headed niches, of a kind known in other Roman baths and probably cupboards. Below them was originally a long seat on stone supports. At the east side of the room opens a latrine, M, with massive buttressed foundation on the steep river bank and sewer lined with a curved troughing in cut stone.

A door in the south wall of the dressing room leads to a vestibule, N, where the floor and the steps to adjacent rooms are much worn. Here the bather, turning east, entered the cold bath-room (*frigidarium*), K, in the middle of which stood a laver for douching; its base is still visible, slotted both for feed-pipe and drain. At the east end is the cold bath, L, later disused and replaced by a much smaller bath, J, on the north.

The south door of the vestibule led into a room of gentle heat (*tepidarium*), E1, warmed by a hypocaust fed from the hotter room, E2, beyond it, and from this warm room a door, later blocked, led eastwards into an anteroom, I, perhaps serving as an *unctorium*, where the bather's skin was rubbed with oil, but certainly insulating

ALTAR TO FORTUNE FROM BATH-HOUSE (CHESTERS MUSEUM).

the main room which it served from the cold air of the cold bath-room. It was warmed with hot air from the hypocaust of the room beyond. The long room, H, began existence as a room of dry-heat (*laconicum*). Its east wall has four external buttresses; its south wall has none, but is four feet six inches thick and built in stages, with a flue leading to the original furnace. The room produced an altar dedicated " To the goddess Fortune, the preserver, Venenus, a German, willingly and deservedly ", its front exhibiting a figure of the deity. The dedicator was presumably a German irregular trooper. Both H and I were later deprived of artificial heating and were filled up with sand to serve as sun-parlours.

From room H the bather passed through another west door, later blocked, into the hot room (*caldarium*), E2. This was the place where he sweated hard, washed in hot water and was scraped with the *strigil*. Hot water was provided from a boiler supported upon the mass of masonry, G, at the south end of the room, under which ran a flue from the furnace beyond.

In this room were found numerous small blocks of calcareous tufa, of which the use was explained by the late

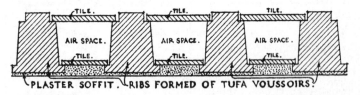

SECTION SHOWING USE OF TUFA VOUSSOIRS IN AN INSULATED BARREL-VAULTED CEILING.

Mr. Parker Brewis. Slightly wedge-shaped, they would, put together, form an arched rib. A number of such ribs set at close intervals, would not only constitute the framework of a barrel-vault, but could carry tiles laid on their upper and lower ledges to form a double ceiling, admirably light in construction and acting as a hot air-jacket to prevent heavy condensation on the walls of the steaming room. The apsed bay, F, projecting westward, contained the hot bath, now removed, though the duct for its outlet pipe remains, and over it comes a splayed window, four feet wide, outside which Roman window-glass was found. Another interesting stone is a trough from the bottom of the latrine sewer, showing the leaded seating for a wire grid or drain-trap.

From the hot room the bather returned to the first warm room to cool, then went through the vestibule into the cold room, K, to bathe or douche in cold water, thus closing the pores and avoiding a chill, and so back to his clothes in the dressing-room.

Two small westward rooms, B and D, are both additional and still to be explained. A Roman bathing establishment normally contained provision for two different kinds of sweat-bathing: one in moist heat, provided in the rooms already described, the other in dry heat. Dry heat, once produced in room H in its original form, was later produced in the north room (*laconicum*), B, heated by a charcoal-furnace and completely clad in wall-flues. Access is from a lobby, D, and this is built over an earlier *laconicum*. Here, as elsewhere in the building, will be noted the massive door-jambs of stone obviating wooden door-frames, which would tend to warp or rot in the varied heat of the baths.

Near the bath-house remains of a large extra-mural settlement have been observed from the air and on the ground to south and west of the fort. Still further south lay the cemetery of the fort, where the river bends rapidly to the east and the sunk fence delimiting the park of Chesters reaches the river bank. A number of monumental slabs have been found at the spot which is a place of peace and beauty.

The road leaving the fort for the south aims for Walwick Grange; south of which the Stanegate crossed the North Tyne below Wall and ran westward to Fourstones, Newbrough and Chesterholm.

FROM CHESTERS TO CARRAWBURGH

For 500 yards west of the fort the Wall runs through private grounds, and then, once more coincident with the Carlisle road, climbs the hill to Walwick. The foundations used often to peep through the road surface when it consisted only of broken stone or macadam; and the accompanying wood-cut was prepared when the surfacing was worn and thunder-showers had removed all dust. In 1928, in similar conditions, the Wall was measured and found to be seven feet seven inches wide, the Broad Foundation extending another two feet two inches beyond it on the south. The Vallum is here well seen in the field on the left. Where the road veers south-west, off the line of the Wall, the platform of milecastle 28 (Walwick) is evident, indicating a long-axis milecastle, just west of the farm-track running south. Walwick Hall is next passed, where the southward view is exceedingly fine, commanding the North and South Tyne valleys, with the Iron-Age hill-fort on Warden Hill between them, while another hill-fort

THE WALL IN THE ROAD BELOW WALWICK, 1862, LOOKING W.N.W.

appears east of the village of Wall and to south-east is seen Hexham, with its priory church. The Carlisle road covers the north mound of the Vallum, and the ditch of the Wall is seen to north in excellent condition. Turret 28a lies about three hundred yards west of Walwick Hall; 28b at the usual distance beyond it.

After a cross-roads, there is a sharp ascent by Tower Tye, a cottage once crenellated, built about 1730 with stones from the Wall. On the crest of this rise the road swings into the Vallum ditch, but soon leaves it for the north mound. Over the summit, milecastle 29 (Tower Tye) is distinctly marked on the north by the hollows made in robbing its walls. Here, as at milecastle 25, are also traces of a ditch. To the south

THE SETTING OF THE ROMAN WALL
—CRAG LOUGH AND WINSHIELDS, LOOKING WEST FROM HOTBANK

THE WALL AT HOUSESTEADS
—LOOKING EAST TOWARDS KING'S CRAG

Photo by
Philipson & Sons Ltd.

of the Vallum, in a fir plantation, is a temporary camp with traverses at its four gates, and further south still a native homestead. To north, a fine piece of Wall, six feet high, is seen running parallel with the road for some distance. In this length turret 29a was uncovered in 1873: it measures internally eleven feet ten inches by eleven feet four inches, has wing-walls to fit the Broad Wall and had monolithic stone

TURRET 29a, BLACK CARTS, 1873.

door jambs, like turrets 26b and 29b. The south wall exhibits only its lowest course, with a doorway three feet wide, but the north wall stands fourteen courses high. The wood-cut represents the turret when first excavated; it is now much more ruinous and overgrown. Beyond the Hen Gap, the break in the Wall for the Simonburn branch-road, the Wall has facing-stones rather larger than usual and halfway up the hill lies turret 29b, excavated in 1912. Its occupation seemed not to extend beyond the close of the second century, though it had not been dismantled. It was approached by a branch track eleven feet wide, leading off at right-angles from the Military Way.

The ditch of the Vallum is rock-cut all the way up the hill, though somewhat overgrown with trees: its temporary crossings are seen at every 45 yards, many apparently half-finished; also gaps in the south mound and, as rarely, in the marginal mound. The serious student will find this sector full of interest. The rock removed from the ditch has mostly been broken up small and packed into the mounds, but four large masses lie on the south berm as they were brought out of the ditch. The easternmost block has holes for the chain-grips that were used to lift it.

At Limestone Corner, on the crest, the northward view is magnificent, across North Tynedale, with Chipchase Castle on its north bank, to the Simonside Hills and Cheviot. Milecastle 30 (Limestone Corner), lies where the stone field-walls meet on the summit. Here for the first time, the Military Way can be plainly detected, coming up to the south gate of the milecastle and then swinging away to run westwards. A hundred yards beyond the milecastle it passes obliquely under the modern road, and climbs on to the north mound of the Vallum, which it occupies as far as Carrawburgh farm house. Excavation has shown that the gaps in the north mound had been filled to carry the Military Way.

The ditches of both Wall and Vallum should now be examined. Both are cut through the very hard quartz dolerite composing the hill, and the excavated masses of stone lie upon their brinks. The huge blocks that the Roman managed to dislodge and lift or roll are particularly well seen in the Wall ditch. On its north lip lies an immense stone, now split into three by frost, which when first removed must have been one single block weighing not less than thirteen tons. In the ditch itself a comparable mass has not yet been shifted, and its upper surface reveals the method of dislodgement, exhibiting a number of holes for insertion of wedges. These holes are all made along the thin veins of quartz which intersect the dolerite, where the wedges, when driven in, would promote cleavage. Iron or wooden wedges were used, the former hammered, the latter expanded by watering. Two such iron wedges found in the Wall structure at milecastle 26 have steel-faced tips and soft heads for hammering. The quarrying, by means of such wedges, and lifting, by means of cranes, was heavy work, but Roman engineers were well accustomed to do it.

East of the unmoved mass of rock the Wall ditch is wholly unfinished, probably at the end of a season's work. Contrari-wise, the Vallum ditch is fully dug, except opposite the mile-castle, where there is an original causeway of undisturbed rock. For the Vallum, the ditch was the essential thing, while to the Wall it was an accessory. Here too, for about 100 yards beyond the milecastle causeway, the Vallum is in its original state, unmodified by gaps or crossings, a very rare condition, occurring elsewhere at Coombe Crag, west of milecastle 51. South of the plantation and about 100 yards from the road, on the summit of the hill, is a temporary camp about fifty-five yards square, with rampart, ditch, gateways and traverses all visible, from which there is a fine view of the South Tyne and the Pennines, with Cross Fell in the far distance. Excavations in 1912 revealed inside this camp a number of paved areas representing the floors of tents or huts. Associated pottery dated this occupation, which was not necessarily the first, to the third century.

Next follow the sites of turrets 30a and 30b, excavated in 1912, and then the farm of Carrawburgh. Here the marginal mound, which has been running along the south lip of the Vallum ditch, stops, and four consecutive causeways are seen in the ditch. The Military Way continues to run on the north mound. Just west of a small quarry on the south comes the site of milecastle 31 (Carrawburgh), and shortly afterwards the fort of BROCOLITIA.

FORT VII   CARRAWBURGH (BROCOLITIA)

The site of this fort, about three and a half miles from Chesters, is a bold platform, guarding both the valley of the Newbrough Burn and an easy approach from the north, along

the west rim of North Tynedale. It measures some 460 feet from north to south and 360 feet from east to west over its ramparts, and covers about three and a half acres. Its ancient name was BROCOLITIA, meaning "Brockholes", and it was garrisoned by the First cohort of Batavians in the third and fourth centuries and earlier by the First cohort of Cugernians and First cohort of Aquitanians. The Batavians occur on an inscription A.D. 237.

The fort is well outlined by its rampart and ditch, and its defensive wall, if freed from fallen débris, would stand several feet high. The positions

INSCRIPTION OF A.D. 237, FROM CARRAWBURGH (CHESTERS MUSEUM).

of the east, south and west gateways and the south guardchamber of the last are clearly discernible; also an interval-tower on the west rampart, a little south of the gate. A centurial stone, found in an upper course of its front wall and now in Chesters Museum, states that "the Thruponian century (built) twenty-four feet", doubtless the tower-front.

CENTURIAL STONE FROM CARRAWBURGH FORT (CHESTERS MUSEUM).

The Narrow Wall formed the north wall of the fort, joined by the side-walls at right-angles, as at a milecastle. This implies that the fort is either contemporary with or, more probably, additional to the Narrow Wall. The relation of the fort to the Vallum, however, is unique: for at Carrawburgh the Vallum ditch was proved in 1934 to have been filled up to make way for the fort instead of avoiding it as happens at other forts. Since, then, the fort was not in existence when the Vallum was first dug, it must come late in the series of forts, and this

wins some corroboration from the discovery here of an
inscription of Sextus Iulius Severus, governor soon after
A.D. 130. Very little excavation, however, has been dŏne inside
the fort. The west wall of a granary is exposed to south of the
main cross-street, near the west gate, and monumental stones
lie about, one bearing a fragmentary relief, another a large
phallus.

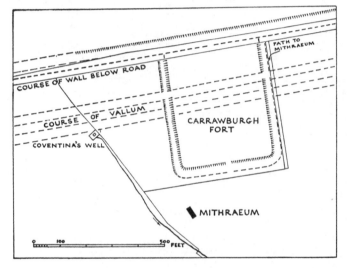

CARRAWBURGH FORT.

The western and southern slope outside the fort have been
covered with the extra-mural buildings of the *vicus,* among
them a bath-house excavated by Clayton in 1873. No attempt
was then made to distinguish periods, but some of the walling
belonged to the fourth century, since coins of the Emperors
Claudius II and Tacitus were found in its core. Its flooring,
of stone slabs, embodied re-used tombstones now at Chesters,
one exhibiting an auxiliary standard-bearer. The plan of the
bath-house is a smaller version of the Chesters plan, suiting
the smaller size of Carrawburgh fort.

At the bottom of the west slope is the swampy source of a
strong spring, in a rectangular basin, recorded by Horsley as
cased with masonry, rediscovered in 1876, and now within a
fence just west of the field-wall: it is usually full of water.
When the structure was excavated by Clayton the top was
choked with stones. Then came a mass of coins, of which

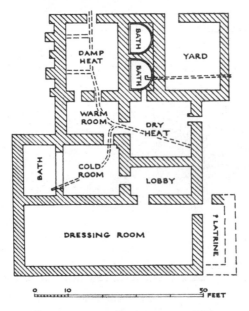

BATH-HOUSE AT CARRAWBURGH, 1873.

many were carried away in a week-end raid upon the site, but
Clayton procured 13,487, four of gold, 184 of silver, and the
rest of bronze, ranging from Mark Antony to Gratian. Next
followed carved stones, altars, more coins, jars and incense-
burners, pearls, brooches and other votive objects in an indis-
criminate mass. The surrounding shrine measured some 40
feet square internally, and there can be little doubt that in
panic or fury its contents had been thrown into the sacred
well, already containing a mass of coins and votive offerings.

The water-goddess was named Coventina and portrayed either singly or in triplicate to express her power.

The coins included at least 327 examples of the smaller

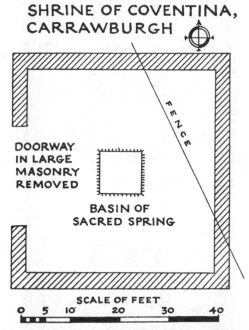

SHRINE OF COVENTINA, CARRAWBURGH

FENCE

DOORWAY
IN LARGE
MASONRY
REMOVED

BASIN OF
SACRED SPRING

SCALE OF FEET
0   5   10   20   30   40

brass denomination (*as*) of Antoninus Pius, which commemorates the pacification of northern Britain after the disturbance of 155. BRITANNIA, disconsolate, sits upon a rock, her hair dishevelled, her head bowed, her banner lowered, her shield cast aside. This dejected figure differs totally from the Britannia of Hadrian (see title-page) or the first Britannia of Pius, who sit armed and alert on a crag, evoking Hadrian's watch between Tyne and Solway or the new frontier drawn by Pius between Forth and Clyde.

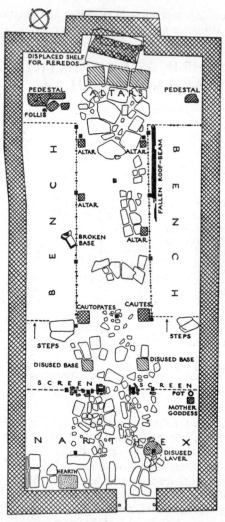

DISPLACED SHELF
FOR REREDOS

PEDESTAL   PEDESTAL

A L T A R S

FOLLIS

B   B
E   E
N   ALTAR   ALTAR   N   FALLEN ROOF-BEAM
C   C
H   ALTAR   H

           BROKEN
           BASE   ALTAR

CAUTOPATES   CAUTES

           STEPS   STEPS

DISUSED BASE   DISUSED BASE

S C R E E N   S C R E E N
                            POT O
                            MOTHER
                            GODDESS

N A R   T   H E X
                        DISUSED
                        LAVER
        HEARTH

CARRAWBURGH MITHRAEUM
FOURTH CENTURY STATE

0   5   SCALE OF FEET   15   20

In 1949, a discovery no less remarkable than Coventina's Well was made during the exceptionally dry summer. Southwest of the fort, on the edge of boggy ground, a building was revealed in the shrinking peat, with three altars to Mithras still standing in position. Excavation showed its long and varied history. Founded shortly after A.D. 205, it was soon enlarged and thereafter twice refurbished during the third century. After the destruction of A.D. 297 it was rebuilt and not long afterwards deliberately desecrated, presumably by a Christian commandant. The altars and sculptures of the final stage are now replaced with cast-stone replicas, the owner, Mr. W. J. Benson, having presented the building to the nation; and a full-scale illuminated model, with commentary, is to be seen and heard in the Museum of Antiquities at Newcastle, where the relics from the shrine are exhibited. Immediately outside the door of the building was a small shrine to the Nymphs and *Genius loci;* further to the southeast a large hollow in the hillside indicates yet another important structure.

Under three miles south of Carrawburgh lies Newbrough, on the Stanegate; where, at the church of St. Peter Stonecroft, is a Roman fort site, revealed by excavation in 1930. The Stanegate then follows the modern road past Grindon Hill, west of which three Roman temporary camps are to be found on its south side.

FROM CARRAWBURGH TO HOUSESTEADS

West of Carrawburgh the Wall continues below the road past the farm house of Carraw, formerly a grange of the priors of Hexham. A quarter of a mile farther on the platform of milecastle 32 (Carraw) is visible south of the road; at normal distance beyond, lies the site of turret 32*a*. Nearly half a mile to south a small Roman camp, called Brown Dykes, occupies a hill-top with extensive prospect. A smaller camp, 300 yards E.N.E. of it, is hardly visible. The mounds and ditch of the Vallum and the ditch of the Wall are here very grand and very close to each other; the Vallum continues straight, while the Wall swings slightly southwards,

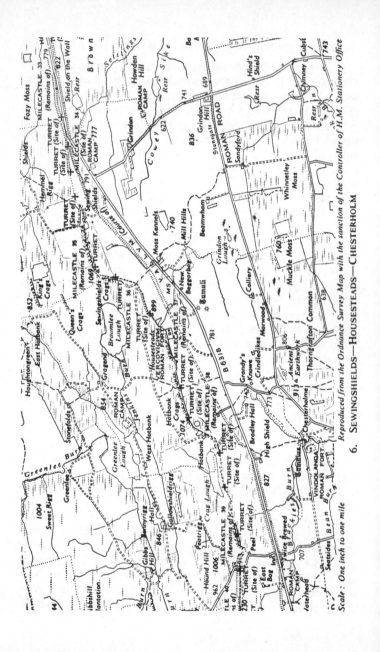

6. SEWINGSHIELDS—HOUSESTEADS—CHESTERHOLM

Scale: One inch to one mile

Reproduced from the Ordnance Survey Map with the sanction of the Controller of H.M. Stationery Office

avoiding a bog on the north, and securing the crown of the
hill, where it bends slightly to the north. The road keeps to
the south, parallel with the Vallum, and in the field to north,
milecastle 33 (Shield-on-the-Wall) is evident. Its north wall
and gate, of type II, with larger backward projection than
usual, are in good condition; while south of the stone wall,
which divides two estates, slight remains of the milecastle's
south gateway are to be seen, including its monolithic threshold. Here too the Wall ditch is remarkably bold.

Still further west, the cottage of Shield-on-the-Wall lies
on the south and beyond it a reservoir, supplying the Settling-
stones barytes mine. Ahead the ridge of the Whin Sill, geo-
logically described as an intrusive mass of quartz dolerite,
along which the Wall runs in the central part of its course,
comes boldly into view. Four successive crests are in sight,
which belong to a single escarpment and seem to chase each
other to the north.

After the twenty-seventh milestone, 150 yards west of the
site of turret 33a, the modern road takes to the south of
both Wall and Vallum, at the bridge across the Coesike. The
Wall and Vallum also part company; the Vallum running
along the " tail " of the hill so that its ditch need not be cut
in the hard whinstone; the Wall, aiming uphill for Sewingshields farm house, has been rooted out to furnish building
stones for the house and field walls. The ditch accompanies
it to milecastle 34 (Grindon), marked by a clump of trees,
and then ends abruptly, the height of the cliffs to westward
rendering it unnecessary. The Military Way leaves the north
mound of the Vallum and runs more or less parallel to the
Wall. Now, to quote Hutton, we " quit the beautiful scenes
of cultivation, and enter upon the rude of nature, and the
wreck of antiquity ".

Milecastle 34 is of type II, assigned to the Twentieth
Legion by the inscription of milecastle 47. At the next field-
wall beyond the milecastle is the site of turret 34a, found in
1913; and north of the Wall two sites of interest lay opposite
milecastle 34 and north-east of Sewingshields farmhouse
respectively. The first was an ancient inhabited site on an

island in Fozey Moss; the second was Sewingshields Castle, called by Sir Walter Scott, in *Harold the Dauntless* (canto 6), the Castle of Seven Proud Shields.

When Dr. Lingard was there, its walls were five feet high. Later, the vaults were removed and the whole area ploughed. Scott described this state of affairs romantically

> . . . . " No towers are seen
> On the wild heath, but those that Fancy builds,
> And, save a fosse that tracks the moor with green,
> Is nought remains to tell of what may there have been."

But a more striking tale was preserved by the Rev. John Hodgson and Miss Carlyle.

"Immemorial tradition has asserted that King Arthur, his queen Guenever, court of lords and ladies, and his hounds, were enchanted in some cave of the crags, or in a hall below the Castle of Sewing-shields, and would continue entranced there till some one should first blow a bugle-horn that laid on a table near the entrance into the hall, and then, with ' the sword of the stone,' cut a garter also placed there beside it. But none had ever heard where the entrance to this enchanted hall was, till the farmer at Sewingshields, about fifty years since, was sitting knitting on the ruins of the castle, and his clew fell, and ran downwards through a rush of briars and nettles, as he supposed, into a deep subterranean passage. Full in the faith, that the entrance into King Arthur's hall was now discovered, he cleared the briary portal of its weeds and rubbish, and entering a vaulted passage, followed, in his darkling way, the thread of his clew. The floor was infested with toads and lizards: and the dark wings of bats, disturbed by his unhallowed intrusion, flitted fearfully around him. At length his sinking faith was strengthened by a dim, distant light, which, as he advanced, grew gradually brighter, till all at once, he entered a vast and vaulted hall, in the centre of which a fire without fuel, from a broad crevice in the floor, blazed with a high and lambent flame, that showed all the carved walls, and fretted roof, and the monarch, and his queen and court, reposing around in a theatre of thrones and costly couches. On the floor, beyond the fire, lay the faithful and deep-toned pack of thirty couple of hounds; and on a table before it, the spell-dissolving horn, sword, and garter. The shepherd reverently but firmly grasped the sword, and as he drew it leisurely from its rusty scabbard, the eyes of the monarch and his courtiers began to open, and they rose till they sat upright. He cut the garter; and, as the sword was being slowly sheathed, the spell assumed its antient power, and they all gradually sunk to rest; but not before the monarch had lifted up his eyes and hands, and exclaimed,

> ' O woe betide that evil day,
> On which this witless wight was born,
> Who drew the sword—the garter cut,
> But never blew the bugle-horn! '

. . . . Terror brought on loss of memory, and he was unable to give any correct account of his adventure, or the place where it occurred."

Yet another local tradition of King Arthur attaches to the high points called the King's and Queen's Crag, half a mile north-west of Sewingshields, beyond the Wall:

"King Arthur, seated on the farthest rock, was talking with his queen, who, meanwhile, was engaged in arranging her ' back hair.' Some expression of the queen's having offended his majesty, he seized a rock which lay near him, and with an exertion of strength for which the Picts were proverbial, threw it at her, a distance of about a quarter of a mile! The queen, with great dexterity, caught it upon her comb, and thus warded off the blow; the stone fell about midway between them, where it lies to this very day, with the marks of the comb upon it, to attest the truth of the story. The stone probably weighs about twenty tons! "

Between Queen's Crag and the Wall there are many traces of Roman quarrying, in-cluding wedge holes in the rock.

Turret 34b lay amid the farm-buildings of Sewingshields, where a centurial stone is pre-served, of " The century of Gellius Philippus ".

CENTURIAL STONE, AT SEWINGSHIELDS.

After a walk westwards through a small plantation, the columnar formation of the dolerite rock soon attracts atten-tion: it cleaves easily and tends to break off, and every thunderstorm throws down some of the cliff. Now follows Cat's Gate, a narrow chasm by which, says local tradition, the Scots crept under the Wall. Milecastle 35 (Sewingshields), much robbed for repairs to the farm house, lies some 540 yards west of it, and had gates of type II. A hundred yards before the summit comes the site of turret 35a and from the top are seen Broomlee Lough, to west, the smaller Grindon Lough, to south of the Carlisle road.

Just beyond the summit a Saxon boundary earthwork, known as the Black Dyke, may be seen running towards the Wall from the north across the moors. From the north the Dyke seems to have run up to the Wall at King's Hill, a little beyond milecastle 36, and followed the Wall to this summit. It consists of a ditch, with its upcast disposed in a mound on the east, so that the work faces west. It runs from the North Tyne at Tarset, across the heads of the westward valleys, to the South Tyne at Moralee.

West of turret 35b comes Busy Gap, where the Wall ditch reappears, as at all such breaks in the escarpment. The triangular enclosure in the gap is post-Roman. On the west side of the gap is a wicket gate through which a drove road passes. This part of the Border long suffered from the incessant wars and raids between England and Scotland, and Busy Gap was a pass much frequented by raiders. A " Busy Gap rogue " was in medieval Newcastle a well-known term of abuse. After Camden and Cotton visited the Wall in 1599, the former wrote, as Philemon Holland translated: " the Wall goeth forward more aslope by Iverton, Forsten, and Chester-in-the-Wall, near to Busy Gap—a place infamous for thieving and robbing; where stood some castles (chesters they call them) as I heard, but I could not with safety take the full survey of it, for the rank robbers thereabouts ".

Milecastle 36 (King's Hill), soon reached, stands on a slope of one in five, and is a long-axis milecastle. Its north gate had been first rebuilt as a postern and finally blocked. Next follow in rapid succession two narrow and rather steep gaps without names, and Kennel Crags, on whose summit stood turret 36a, just east of Knag Burn and the famous fort of Housesteads, Camden's Chester-in-the-Wall.

In the bottom of the valley is a gateway discovered in 1856 which is one of the very rare gates through the Wall, elsewhere than at a milecastle or a fort and was used for civil as opposed to military traffic. There was another at Portgate but nothing is known in detail of its plan. Here the plan is of special interest. It is a single passage flanked by guard-chambers and pivot-holes at back and front show that there were two sets of doors, so that parties could be admitted for examination and the payment of tolls, and allowed through the second door in either direction only when the process was complete. It thus affords a glimpse of Roman frontier control rarely given by archaeology. When originally found, in 1856, the structure yielded coins of Claudius II and Constantius I, and re-excavation in 1936 showed that it had been inserted in the Wall in the fourth century. A similar gateway is known on the African frontier near Gemellae.

The Knag Burn passes under the Wall in a culvert, as it must have done in Roman times. Between the burn and the fort are traces of extra-mural buildings, and the Military Way may be seen winding up to the east gate.

Many visitors will not have walked along the Wall from the Coesike but will have motored along the Carlisle road. Six hundred yards west of the bridge another small, square, temporary camp lies close beside the road, on the south, just before the branch-road to Haydon Bridge. Past the schoolhouse, again on the south, are outcrops of coal from which the Romans probably took the coal used in the fort of Housesteads; there is also an outcrop of limestone which has been much quarried by them.

The farm house of Moss Kennels is next passed on the south of the road, and then the house called Beggar Bog. Just beyond the car-park and the gate leading to Housesteads a round tumulus, probably of the Bronze Age, lies to south of the road, and there is another still further south in the valley.

FORT VIII HOUSESTEADS (VERCOVICIUM)

The ancient name of Housesteads is abbreviated in an inscription as VER, and this establishes VERCOVICIUM for the BORCOVICIUM of the *Notitia*, the initial constants being interchangeable in later Latin. Its garrison in the third and fourth centuries was the First cohort of Tungrians, one thousand strong, reinforced in the third century by the *cuneus Frisiorum*, or formation of Frisian cavalry, and the *numerus Hnaudifridi*, or Notfried's unit of irregulars. In the second century the fort presumably started with a military cohort as garrison, but a legionary holding-garrison is also known. The fort lies four and three-quarter miles from Carrawburgh and covers just over five acres. Its plan is the usual rectangle with rounded angles, 610 by 367 feet in size. Its long axis runs

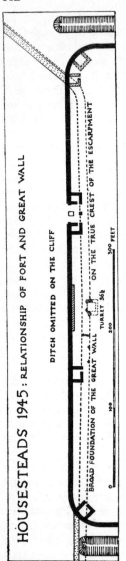

HOUSESTEADS 1945: RELATIONSHIP OF FORT AND GREAT WALL

DITCH OMITED ON THE CLIFF

ON THE TRUE "CREST" OF THE ESCARPMENT

BROAD FOUNDATION OF THE GREAT WALL

TURRET 36½

0   100   200   500 FEET

from east to west, as at no fort so far described, because the fort is planted at the very edge of the cliff, on a narrow shelf which itself slopes sharply southwards. A better site further west was sacrificed in order to overlook the Knag Burn gap, carrying an ancient traffic route from the north.

The site, including Knag Burn gateway and milecastle 37, was bought by the late Professor G. M. Trevelyan in 1930 and presented to the National Trust, which also owns the Wall as far as Peel Crag. The fort is in the guardianship of the Ministry of Public Building and Works.

The Narrow Wall joins the fort at its rounded north angles. It is evident that the fort was then already erected, because its north-east angle-tower was actually moved (see p. 117) to suit the final arrangement. But, before any fort was built at all, the foundations of the Broad Wall and of turret 36b had been laid out on the crest, and their demolished remains were overlaid by the rampart and *intervallum* road of the fort. The fort was thus added after the Broad foundation had been laid, but before the Narrow Wall had been built. The Vallum passes so far to south as to make no deviation from its straight course. Its ditch, levelled and obliterated by buildings of the Roman extra-mural

THE BATH HOUSE, CHESTERS

Photo by
Philipson & Sons Ltd.

LATRINE AND WATER-TANK AT THE SOUTH
EAST ANGLE, HOUSESTEADS

Photo by
Valentine & Sons Ltd.

settlement, was found 85 yards south of the fort in 1934, and was crossed opposite the south gate by a causeway of living rock.

The plan of the fort is best appreciated by entering the south gate and walking uphill to the centre. There the *via praetoria* leads eastwards from the headquarters building (10, *principia*) to the main gate or *porta praetoria,* while the *via principalis* runs across the fort to the north gate, *porta principalis sinistra,* and south gate, *porta principalis dextra.* The space east of this road was filled with five long narrow barrack-buildings (13-18) and a mess-room (15), with baths, discovered in 1832, at its east end; on the north of the *principia* lie the granaries (8, *horrea*); on the south, the commandant's house (12, *praetorium*). Behind this central row of buildings came a hospital (9, *valetudinarium*) and near them miscellaneous buildings of uncertain purpose (7, 11): then five more barracks (1-3; 5 and 6) and a workshop (4). Then come the west rampart and west gate, *porta decumana.*

A more particular survey may begin by examining the *principia* (see plan). The visible building, which had a front portico, projecting into the street was first built in the Severan age and remains of a Hadrianic *principia* have been found below it. Large masonry at the entrance, from which probably came reliefs of Mars and of Victory now at Chesters, has been robbed away, leaving only a threshold with pivot-hole. The entrance leads into a courtyard bordered on three sides by an open colonnade, later closed by walling. A doorway beyond leads into a hall with eastward aisle and north side-door. In its north-west corner is the packing of a dais (*tribunal*), from which an ornamental front and the top have been removed. Beyond this lie the usual five rooms. The middle one is the shrine of the standards, and beds are cut in the stones flanking its threshold, to receive low stone screens, as seen at Chesterholm. In the record-room, to north, heated by a hypocaust, were found over 800 iron arrow-heads with fragments of wooden shafts: the place had thus finally become an armoury. The pay-room, to south, ceased in the end to be two, and a new wall at its back cut off space for a lavatory. The paymaster, who was the regimental standard-bearer, was now living in his office.

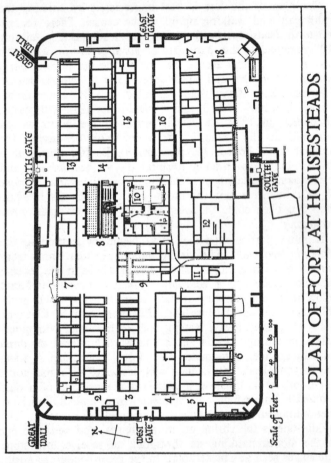

PLAN OF FORT AT HOUSESTEADS

North of the headquarters building lie two granaries side by side. These are buttressed buildings, whose floors, now removed, rested on a ventilated basement in which rows of

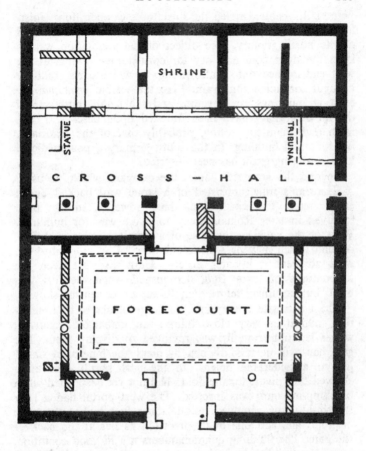

SHRINE

STATUE

TRIBUNAL

C R O S S - H A L L

F O R E C O U R T

0   10   70 FEET

PLAN OF SEVERAN HEADQUARTERS, HOUSESTEADS. LATER ADDITIONS ARE SHADED.

piers, still visible, carried the joists of a wooden floor. Joist-holes are seen opposite each row of piers, in the south wall of the north granary. The object of the ventilation was to keep the floor cool and dry for corn-storage. Doors at the west end opened onto platforms up to which carts could be brought for unloading grain. Like the visible *principia,* the existing buildings are Severan, and the south buttresses of the north granary have been founded upon bases and caps from a dismantled portico, probably that of the Hadrianic headquarters building. In the south granary a post-medieval kiln for drying grain has been inserted.

Beyond the granaries comes the rampart, which, as usual in Hadrian's time, consisted of a stone wall backed by an earth bank. The earth bank has, however, mostly been removed in later Roman times, to make way for buildings. West of the gateway the base of a staircase ramp is visible, beyond which may be seen foundations of an interval-tower, with adjacent rain-water cistern. Here also are seen the foundations of turret 36*b*, demolished when the fort was built, but occupied before demolition, as its hearths show.

The north gate is very fine, the large blocks of its founda-tion exhibiting very close joints: an embanked roadway, which led out from it, was removed to display them. The gate has twin portals, divided by piers, the innermost stand-ing to considerable height. In the east portal excavation showed that pivots for the doors had not yet been fitted when blocking-masonry was inserted. The west portal had a later threshold, now removed, about three feet higher than the original one, and one of its pivot-blocks lies at the back of the gate. The flanking guardchambers are in good condition, and, in rebuilding the west one, part of an altar to Jupiter was used as a walling stone and is now in Chesters Museum. Outside this chamber is a large water-tank. Its stone sides, themselves of re-used material, were run in with lead in vertical slots at the joints and cramped with iron at the top. Their tops are worn by sharpening swords or by washing clothes, as in tanks found in more than one Roman fort. Many tanks at Housesteads are related to the towers, collecting water from their flat roofs; for here water is not plentiful below ground and rain-water became particularly valuable.

At the north-east angle the Narrow Wall abuts on the fort at the north end of the curve. When the Wall came, the tower already in normal position in the middle of the curve was pulled down and re-erected at the junction as now visible. The foundations of the original tower have also been discovered but are not displayed, though the patching executed when its walls were pulled away from the fort-wall can still be seen.

Further south, behind the east rampart, an interval-tower lies midway between the angle and the gate. The high level of its floor shows that the existing structure is a rebuilding, and just north of it there is another large water-tank, at an earlier and lower level.

At the east gate (*porta praetoria*) the foundation-work carrying the external wall of the south tower is worth note. The south portal has been blocked, but not before its threshold and pivot-blocks were renewed under Severus, as seen on the north side: the blocking therefore presumably belongs to after A.D. 297. When blocked, the portal became a guard-chamber, while the older guardchamber to south became a coal-store, in which nearly a cart-load of coal was found, no doubt won from local out-crops (see p. 111). Two successive holes, in which iron cups for the door-pivots were fixed, remain on the north side, and one on the south. The stone stop-block for the doors is also seen, and Roman wheel-ruts, eight inches deep, appear in the checked threshold. Like the ruts at Pompeii, they approximate closely to the British railway gauge, but this does not mean that George Stephenson took his gauge from Roman practice. His standard had in fact been reached, by averaging the wheel-gauge of a hundred carts, some years before these gates were uncovered.

On the north side of the *via praetoria*, leading west from this gate, is a long building (15) of massive construction, with buttresses; excavation in 1961 showed that it began with some men's quarters, like barrack-rooms, and that these

were rebuilt in a fashion after A.D. 197. The existing building, of the early fourth century, was a buttressed stores-
building accessible to carts. The bath-block at its east end
looks like a still later insertion. The fourth-century structure
is built of exceptionally long stones, with feather-tooling. In
the bath-suite can be seen a bath and voussoirs from an
insulated double ceiling, as at Chesters. To north lay barrack
14, excavated in 1959-60 and in part displayed. The Hadrianic

THRESHOLD OF NORTH PORTAL, EAST GATE, HOUSESTEADS: LOOKING
WEST. THE RIGHT-HAND OR NORTH RUT IS NOW BROKEN.

building, with veranda and projecting centurion's quarters,
had ten barrack-rooms under one roof. Little remained of its
Severan successor, but the Constantian building had seven
barrack-rooms and a workshop, all built as separate units,
of the kind seen again at Greatchesters. Later modifications
were few and coins went down to Gratian's issue of 367-375.
The corresponding barrack to north was, like this one,
excavated in 1898, but has been filled in again.

South of the east gate, a staircase ramp is attached to the
inner side of the fort-wall. On the outside, large blocks are
seen at the tower positions, as if these had been built first
as separate units. An interval-tower of late date is also seen.
The south-west angle-tower is well-preserved and masked by
a very fine water-tank, blocking its doorway. The tank was

originally lead-lined and its stone sides are still jointed with lead flashings and iron cramps. At least two more such tanks lay close by on the north, as shown on photographs in the Museum.

The over-flow from the tanks was used to flush the men's latrine, a rectangular building with a long axial passage, on each side of which seats were arranged over two deep sewers. A stone channel in front of them carried running water for washing sponges, the Roman substitute for toilet-paper, and at one end is a stone basin for washing hands. The outfall-sewer disappears under the rampart, to discharge at a point as yet unknown, further down the hillside.

More barracks lay to north and an interval-tower is seen on the south. Then comes the south gate, a massive structure with two portals, pivot-holes for the doors and a guard-chamber on each side. The east portal was once walled up, and it is now known that this happened in the fourth century. In the thirteenth century, a Border farmer built outside the east guardchamber a vaulted undercroft with central pier, and in the guardchamber itself is a later corn-drying kiln. The lower part of the eastern external steps to the upper living-room is less easy to see.

Stone lintels with arched heads were used to crown windows or doorways of gate-towers, and several lie here, ornamented with circular or cruciform designs, the latter without Christian significance. Inside the fort and near this gate were found, in 1853, a gold ear-drop, a gold signet-ring with paste *intaglio* of Mercury, and a *sestertius* of Commodus dated to A.D. 181, perhaps lost during the disaster of A.D. 197 and now at Chesters Museum.

Between the south gate and *principia* are the fragmentary remains of the commandant's courtyard house (12), of which the north wing, sheltered by the slope, is best preserved; the others are denuded. A smaller building (9), immediately behind the *principia,* has been identified as a hospital, efficiently planned with small side-wards opening off a corridor running round a central light-well.

The south rampart is in good preservation, ten courses

high. At the south-west angle the tower front is built with
larger stones, as already noted in other towers. Just north of
the angle-tower a long staircase-ramp extends to the next
interval-tower, which has again been erected before the
fort-wall and contains an oven.

The west rampart is still eleven courses high and has a
bonding-course of stone slabs, while the west gate stands

THE WEST GATE, HOUSESTEADS, FROM THE WEST, SHOWING
BLOCKING WALLS IN BOTH PORTALS, NOW REMOVED.

higher than any. Its north impost remains to full height,
ready for the cap and springer seen at the main east gate of
Birdoswald. In the outer central pier, holes and slots for the
bar of the doors are visible, with corresponding holes behind
the imposts. The threshold and stop-block in the south portal
belong to the Severan reconstruction, after which this portal
was blocked, presumably under Constantius about A.D. 297.
The north portal was blocked with rougher masonry, probably in the reconstruction of A.D. 369. Bruce's wood-cut, here
retained, shows the different character of the work. The guardchambers were later converted into heated rooms, as at the
east gate of Birdoswald.

The inner face of the west rampart, to both north and

south of the gate, exhibits several additional buildings, but no interval-tower now appears to north. The fort between the west rampart and *via quintana* was occupied by five barracks (1-3, 5 and 6) and, on the south side of the westward road, a workshop and smithy (4).

Like the north-east angle, the north-west angle of the fort antedates the Narrow Wall, which makes contact with the front of a normal angle-tower. Excavation has shown, however, that the west ditch cut into the Broad foundation while leaving space for the Narrow Wall to pass between its end and the cliff. The Museum lies to south-west of the fort and houses a most interesting collection of objects, models and photographs.

To south and east of the fort there are widespread visible remains of Roman extra-mural buildings, indicating a *vicus* or settlement of no small size. Early antiquaries were astonished both at the extent of the buildings and at the number of inscribed and sculptured stones on the slopes and in the valley; while air-photography today confirms the number and variety of the buildings. Just outside the south gate are very massive foundations, and a group of shops or taverns, erected upon terraces and distinguished by their sills grooved for shuttered fronts. Excavation has shown that the settlement dates, in its most highly-developed form, to the third and fourth centuries, and an inscription indicates that, like all such settlements, it had local self-government. The place was not without sensation: in one tavern, now called in local fashion " Murder House ", a male skeleton, with a knife-point in its rib, was found buried in the back room.

The bath-house of the fort once stood on a rocky shelf to east of the Knag Burn, opposite the middle of the fort. It was heated by hypocausts, with soot still in the flues. Though it was ransacked many years ago, to supply stones for neighbouring field-walls, fragments of walling hint at remains still worth examination. Nearer the Wall is a fenced spring, cased in Roman masonry, which seems to have supplied the establishment. Opposite the baths, and to west of the burn, was found a Roman lime-kiln.

South of the *vicus* and the marshy valley rises the ridge called Chapel Hill. Beyond its west end, close to an active spring, lay a half-underground temple, dedicated to Mithras and first discovered in 1822. Excavations of 1898 revealed a

RELIEF OF MITHRAS, PIERCED FOR ILLUMINATION FROM BEHIND, FROM HOUSESTEADS (NEWCASTLE).

long narrow nave, flanked by benches for reclining wor- shippers. Beyond it was the sanctuary which yielded an altar dedicated in the consulship of Gallus and Volusianus, in A.D. 252; also the very notable relief of Mithras rising from the rock, surrounded by the signs of the Zodiac; and, finally, statues of his attendant deities of light and darkness. The relief was so designed and placed that it could be illuminated from the back, thus revealing Mithras encircled in light. A small altar to Jupiter, Cocidius and the guardian deity of the locality, re-used in the *mithraeum* and originally erected by

DEO

SOLI·INVI
CTOMITRÆ
SAECVLARI
LITORIVS
PACATIANⁿˢ
F·COS·PRO
SE ET SVIS·V·S·
·L·M

DEO
MARTI
THINCSO
ET DVABVS
AAISIAGIS
BEDE·ET·FI
MMILENE
ET·N·AVGGER
M·CIVES·TV
IHANTI
VS L M

ALTAR TO MITHRAS (NEWCASTLE) AND IMPOST FROM THE SHRINE OF MARS THINCSUS (CHESTERS MUSEUM), FROM HOUSESTEADS.

a detachment of the Second Legion acting as garrison, recalls the early Antonine treatment of the fort. The worship of Mithras, the Persian god of light, was introduced from the East into Europe in the first century B.C., and by the third century it flourished greatly in various parts of the Empire, especially among officers, who normally dedicate the altars.

The imposing stones in Chesters Museum dedicated to Mars Thincsus were found on the north side of Chapel Hill. This German deity was attended by pairs of Alaisiagae, female spirits or Valkyries, whose names are given as Beda and Fimmilena, Baudihillia and Friagabis. The shrine also yielded a remarkable arched door-head, on which are carved the god and male attendants, represented as Mars with

Victories. Their worshippers belong to two irregular units, the *cuneus Frisiorum* and the *numerus Hnaudifridi,* forming part of the third-century garrison. Excavation in 1961 at the site of discovery yielded foundations of a round third-century shrine, 13 feet in internal diameter. At Chesters is also seen a fragment of an elaborate Diocletianic building-inscription from Housesteads, the only one found in a Wall-fort, apart from Birdoswald.

ALTAR TO
THE GOD
HUETER,
FROM
HOUSE-
STEADS
(NEW-
CASTLE).

The sculptures which Housesteads has produced are among the best in the frontier-forts. Those of Mithras and Mars Thincsus have already been noted. But the seated mother-goddesses, found in the *vicus* and now in Newcastle, equal any in the north of England. Even more striking are the reliefs of Victory and of Mars, forming a pair, which came from the front of the *principia* and are now in Chesters Museum. In Housesteads Museum are also seen a very remarkable relief of three divine beings in hooded cloaks, a well carved figure of Mercury, and a bold panel of Hercules and the Nemaean Lion, all from the *vicus*. The most important object from the fort is the Severan building-inscription.

The cemetery lay beyond the extra-mural settlement, and in the low ground to east human remains have been found in draining, while tombstones have been discovered to south.

Like Chesters, Housesteads was connected with the Stanegate, and MacLauchlan surveyed a road running south-east from the fort to the Stanegate at Grindon, which Bruce had no difficulty in tracing from near Moss Kennels farm house to Grindon Shields. Horsley thought that a second road went southwest to the Stanegate near Chesterholm.

FROM HOUSESTEADS TO MILKING GAP

In walking westwards, those who wish to avoid fatigue will best take the Roman Military Way, lined with Roman buildings west of the fort. It is easily found, because all the field-gates are placed upon it; and no-one should need to be reminded to close the gates after him in this land of flocks and herds.

Those who choose to walk along the Wall leave the fort by the west gate and make north-west for a small plantation. The Wall is cleared of tumbled stones on either side, and it is interesting to compare the masonry thus exposed, but not renovated, with that of the Wall west of milecastle 37, which was extensively repaired when freed from fallen material in the nineteenth century; or, again, with the Wall as consolidated by the Ministry of Public Building and Works, which is firm and good when time has removed its first new look. For many visitors this walk will be the most memorable item in their tour: for here in particular can be re-created by every imaginative soul the conditions of the watch and ward which the Romans kept.

The Wall differs slightly in width in different places, as is shown by the offsets and insets of a few inches on the south face. This is due to different gangs working simultaneously on different parts of the line, the centurion in charge of each exercising, within narrow limits, his own judgement as to the width of the Wall. The north face of the Wall, however, is everywhere flush.

At 450 yards from Housesteads comes milecastle 37 (Housesteads), excavated in 1853, 1907 and 1933. It measures internally fifty-seven feet seven inches from east to west, and forty-nine feet seven inches from north to south, with side-walls nine feet thick. The north wall was laid out to Broad

gauge at the north gate, and thence tapered to Narrow gauge
at either side, a treatment not found anywhere else. The south
corners are rounded externally and squared on the inside.
In building this milecastle's wall, two courses of thin sandstone slabs have been used for bonding, as at Housesteads,
much as tiles are used in many Roman structures. If a third
represented the base of the rampart-walk it would give a wall
15 feet high, of which the crenellation would need 5 feet more.
This fits well the north gate, ten feet wide, of most substantial
masonry, where the springers of the arch are in position, and
several arch-stones lie upon the ground, inviting restoration.
Each stone has a lewis-hole in it, so placed that the stone
would hang on the crane at the angle which it was to occupy
in the arch. The jambs, from the floor to the top of the
impost, are a little under six feet high, the arch giving five
feet more of head-room. That the gate was built first, before
the adjacent walling, is shown by the raking joints seen on
both sides in the south face. Under Severus, the gateway was
narrowed to three feet nine inches, and the floor of this later
postern, three feet six inches above the sill of the original,
covered a set of secondary pivot-blocks. The south gateway,
now in poor state, had also been reduced to a postern.

These alterations explain the layers revealed by excavation.
At foundation level, within the north gate, mason's chippings
and a mason's chisel were discovered, and these belong to the
initial construction. Upon the chippings, near the walls, had
been laid a first floor of flags. To west of the axial road a
wooden stores-shed was built and to east a stone barrack of
two rooms, the south unoccupied and used for arms, the north
serving as living-quarters and associated with Hadrianic
pottery. Next, above a levelled mass of stones and rubbish,
came a second floor belonging to the visible building, once
butting against the main walls. A devastation is thus evident
and is in fact the destruction by the Maeatae in A.D. 197. An
attempt was then made to overthrow the jambs of the north
gate. It failed; but they were moved out of perpendicular and
so remain, with the masonry of the Severan postern-gate built
up against them. Structural evidence for fourth-century

occupations had been removed, but pottery later than A.D. 369 was recognised in 1933.

The most valuable relic found in 1853 was a fragment of the inscription commemorating the original building of this milecastle by the Second Legion under Hadrian's legate, Aulus Platorius Nepos. When complete, it was the same as those from milecastles 38 and 42. The stone was re-used in flooring of the Severan period and is much worn. At the foot of the cliff was found an altar dedicated to the Cumberland war-god, Cocidius; and another, to Jupiter, was found south of the milecastle.

In the gap between Housesteads Crags and Cuddy's Crag the Wall ditch is again supplied. From the top of Cuddy's Crag there is a well-known view back to Housesteads and Sewing-shields (frontispiece). Then come Rapishaw Gap and Hotbank Crags. Immediately on gaining the ridge is found the site of turret 37*a*. This turret, like all others in this craggy sector, was demolished under Severus, the Wall being rebuilt and carried

LEFT-HAND BOTTOM CORNER OF HADRIANIC DEDICATION-SLAB, MILECASTLE 37 (HOUSESTEADS), IN CHESTERS MUSEUM.

across its site. In the valley to south the Vallum is seen to be overlooked at close range by high ground on each side. Hesketh Hodgson, an excavator of the nineties, noted how this siting disposed of the theory of the Vallum as a defensive earthwork against the south, remarking that " bar gunpowder, a party of schoolboys could stone the best troops in the world out of the Vallum ".

The view from the summit is extensive and fine. To north, four loughs, Broomlee, Greenlee, Crag, and Grindon, are in sight. The ridge between the first two was extensively quarried by the Romans and a small temporary camp occupies its west end. Beyond the waste, to north-east, lie the Simonside Hills and then Cheviot. The heather-clad hill immediately to south is Barcombe, another quarry-area from which the

Romans won stone. West of Barcombe the gorge leading to the South Tyne is seen and the platform of the fort at Chesterholm, which guarded it, is conspicuously green. South of the Tyne, Langley castle lies near the angle of a large plantation; beyond it are the chimneys of the disused smelt-mills. The valley of the river Allen is seen joining the South Tyne; and a little above their confluence are the ruins of Staward pele, east of the Allen. To south-west lie the Pennine summits of Cross Fell and Cold Fell, with Lakeland Skiddaw and Saddleback emerging from behind the latter.

HADRIANIC DEDICATION-SLAB FROM MILECASTLE 38 (HOTBANK):
FRAGMENTS AT DURHAM AND NEWCASTLE CONJOINED.

At the west end of the crag, beyond the site of turret 37*b*, Crag Lough comes into full view, adding much to the wild beauty of this interesting region. Water-hens build among the reeds at its west end, and wild duck and swans diversify its surface. In Milking Gap milecastle 38 (Hotbank) is evident, in the field opposite Hotbank farm. This milecastle, excavated in 1935, measures internally 50 feet from north to south by 62 feet from east to west. Its gates, of type I with renewed pivot-blocks, were reduced to posterns in the Severan reconstruction, when a tombstone was used as a pivot-block. Pottery of the late fourth century was found. The broken inscribed slab shown in the figure also came from this milecastle. Its left-hand half, now in the Chapter Library at Durham, has no provenance; the right-hand half, now at Newcastle, was built up in the farm house of Bradley, only a quarter of a mile to south-east. It records building by the

Second legion, under Aulus Platorius Nepos as governor of Britain, in A.D. 122-6. But a second and more perfect example, still retaining traces of red paint in its letters, also came from Hotbank; for in 1757 a local correspondent wrote to Stukeley that it " was found at a *statio per Vallum,* nigh the east end of Craig-loch " and this must mean milecastle 38. It also shows that the north and south gates of milecastles each had a similar inscription. The comparable stones from milecastles 37 and 42 will not be forgotten.

HADRIANIC DEDICATION-SLAB FROM MILECASTLE 38 (HOTBANK) NOW AT NEWCASTLE.

At the bottom of the gap the Wall turns sharply to ascend the west crag, and is accompanied by the ditch across the gap itself.

FORT IX CHESTERHOLM (VINDOLANDA)

About a mile due south of Hotbank is the fort of VINDO-LANDA, the modern Chesterholm, once known as Chesters-Iverton or Chesters-on-Caudley. To reach it, take a farm-road running south to the Carlisle road. Before crossing the Vallum, some rough foundations of whinstones, seen to westward, outline a British village, excavated in 1937, inhabited during the period when the Wall lay open in the Antonine period. The Vallum twists sharply southward, so as to avoid a marsh, as is best seen from the heights. At the Carlisle road walkers will take a field-path past the farm of High Shield into the valley, or motorists the first turn southwards after House-steads car-park. Before coming to the fort, there is a large natural hummock, south of which a Roman milestone stands in its original position beside the Stanegate. The base of another milestone exists on the north side of the road about

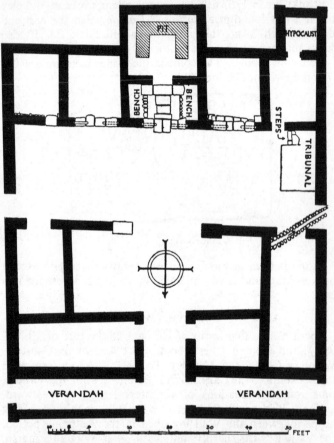

CHESTERHOLM: EARLY FOURTH-CENTURY HEADQUARTERS.

1,700 yards (rather more than a true Roman mile) to west of this; and its shaft, broken up for a gate-post, bore the inscription, in large coarse letters, BONO REIPVBLICAE NATO. " To him who was born for the good of the State ", out of a compliment to the reigning emperor. At Crindledykes, a mile east of Chesterholm and again on the Stanegate, were found in 1885 five complete and two fragmentary milestones; of Severus Alexander (A.D. 223), Probus (A.D. 276-82), Maximinus Caesar (A.D. 305-9), Constantinus Caesar (A.D. 306-7), and Constantinus Augustus (A.D. 307-337). They are now in Chesters Museum.

The Roman name of Chesterholm, VINDOLANDA, is indicated by an inscription from the *vicus* (see p. 132), and the *Notitia* gives the Fourth cohort of Galli as its garrison. The same cohort was in occupation during the third century, but earlier garrisons are unknown.

The fort, covering three and half acres, occupies a prominent platform, sheltered by hills to north and east, and naturally strong on every side but the west, its function being to guard the north-south gap in which it stands. The walls, north gate, west gate and headquarters, excavated by Professor Eric Birley and presented by him to the nation, are now in the custody of the Ministry of Public Building and Works. The central building is a fine example of a fourth-century headquarters, in which the *tribunal* and stone screens of the cross-hall deserve attention; and in the chapel of the standards the unusual pit-like sunken *caisse*, for the chests of the regimental funds, should also be noted. Below this building, which faces north, the discriminating eye can pick out foundations of a third-century headquarters, facing south, which have been constructed in panel-walling between stone piers, like many Roman buildings in Africa.

Excavations have proved that this fort, like primary forts on the Stanegate, was founded by Agricola; and it came to form in due course one of the series of garrison-forts for the first phase of Hadrian's Wall. When the forts were moved from the Stanegate to the Wall, it was not retained in commission, but was occupied once more from A.D. 163 till the close of the century. Under Severus it was laid out afresh as a large and architecturally pretentious fort, facing south. A declaration of loyalty to Caracalla in A.D. 213 by the Fourth cohort of Gauls is now in Housesteads Museum. The existing fort, however, is a complete reconstruction by Constantius I, and faces north: and there were extensive repairs in A.D. 369. There is here a possibility of late occupation; the inscribed tombstone of Brigomaglos, found near the site, has the language and lettering of a sub-Roman Christian monument of the fifth century.

The house in the valley was first built by the Rev. Anthony Hedley, an early nineteenth-century antiquary. An altar discovered in the fort by him is now at Chesters. On one side of it are an axe, a knife, and the ox-victim; on the other the jug for holding the libation and a dish for pouring it. The inscription is translated as: " Sacred to the Genius of the *praetorium;* Pituanius Secundus, prefect of the Fourth cohort of Gauls (erected this)." The *praetorium* was the commandant's house; and the altar was unearthed from its ruins.

ALTAR FROM THE COMMANDANT'S HOUSE (*praetorium*), CHESTERHOLM (CHESTERS MUSEUM).

West of the fort lay a considerable *vicus* or civil settlement. It contained many buildings, lining a street curving round from the west gate to the Stanegate, including an extensive bath-house, now almost obliterated, supplied with water by a stone conduit, partly laid bare. The *vicani Vindolandesses,* as a self-governing community, set up an altar, now in Chesters Museum, found 120 yards west of the fort.

At Chesterholm, if the day is clear and the bull not about, the summit of Barcombe affords an excellent view of Wall, Vallum and Stanegate. Roman quarries will be noted. East of the " Langstane ", a small bronze arm-purse was found in a quarry reopened in 1835, carefully deposited beneath stone-chippings. It contained sixty-three coins, apparently wrapped in leather. Three are of gold, the rest of silver. The *aurei* belong to Claudius, Nero and Vespasian; of the *denarii* nine are republican, the rest imperial, extending from Nero, with seventeen of Trajan and four of Hadrian. The high proportion and excellent preservation of this last group indicates that the coins were laid aside and lost early in Hadrian's reign, when the quarry was being worked for building the Wall.

ALTAR FROM CHESTERHOLM, ERECTED BY THE *vicani Vindolandenses* (CHESTERS MUSEUM).

North of this quarry and north-east of the Langstane, on a shoulder which commands a view of the Wall from Sewingshields to the Nine Nicks of Thirlwall, is a British fortification, with rampart tolerably complete, and, in its north-west corner, a Roman signal-station, linking Chesterholm with points east and west.

FROM MILKING GAP TO GREATCHESTERS

West of Milking Gap, the majestic cliffs, their magnificent columnar formation towering above the lake, afford as romantic a setting as any on the line of the Wall. Turret 38a is halfway up the rise west of the gap; 38b on the summit of Highshield Crag, above the west end of Crag Lough.

On the east edge of the next gap the Wall has been conserved by the Ministry of Public Building and Works, showing how, on the steep descent, the coursing is kept horizontal and is stepped downhill. The method of building the core is also well seen. After a course of rubble has been placed slantwise a layer of mortar has been laid and then another course

BRONZE ARM-PURSE FROM BARCOMBE QUARRY, THORNGRAFTON (CHESTERS MUSEUM).

of stones. This hard white mortar is of the Severan reconstruction and astonishingly tenacious. The Wall now ascends steeply again, turning sharply north on to a high hummock, from which it drops into the gap of Castle Nick, so named from milecastle 39, which was uncovered by Clayton in 1854. The milecastle measures internally fifty feet from east to west, and sixty-two feet from north to south. The side walls, seven feet thick, are in excellent preservation, with six or seven courses of stone standing. The gateways, of type II, are built of small stones, probably to avoid carting large blocks to this comparatively inaccessible site. Excavation in 1908 showed that the gates, after a previous renewal of pivot-blocks, had been reduced to posterns in the Severan reconstruction, as is still seen at the south gate. Foundations of a small barrack-block remain on the west side. The Military Way may also be studied to advantage, as it negotiates the climb out of the gap to east and west.

After another small eminence, another break in the ridge occurs, called Cat Stairs. Here it is possible and convenient to view the crags from the north, by going down Cat Stairs, and walking along the flats to the north of the Wall as far as the next gap at Peel Crag.

On Peel Crag the Wall is again conserved. Here turret 39*a*, excavated in 1911, was found to have been abandoned and dismantled after the disaster of 197, and its recess built up, as were all others in this sector. The large stones of this building-up can still be seen in the south face of the Wall. The cutting and embanking of the Military Way, as it approaches the gap from the east, are well worth study.

In Peel Gap the ditch is again supplied, and runs as far as Winshields milecastle. Both it and the Wall here, splendidly conserved, form a bold re-entrant, making both the climb and the defence easier. It is likely that the low ground north of the Wall was a swamp in Roman days. The road now passing through the gap leads to Kielder, and so into Scotland, but soon degenerates into a mere track.

To south, on the Carlisle road, is the " Once Brewed " Youth Hostel. The modern " Twice Brewed " inn lies a little west of the Youth Hostel. Before the Newcastle and Carlisle railway, however, the present farm of East Twice Brewed was the inn, much frequented by carriers who plied between the two cities. Up to twenty men and fifty horses used to put up there for the night. Hutton had great difficulty in getting a bed, without sharing it with one or more carters; and, at supper, concluded that they had no barricades in their throats, and that eating was the chief end of man.

For a mile and a quarter, from High Shield, the Carlisle road has been running along the south berm of the Vallum. At the Twice Brewed the Vallum swerves northward and begins slowly to converge upon the Wall.

On the west side of Peel Crag formerly stood the farm of Steel Rigg, and close to its site is turret 39*b*, excavated in 1909 and shown to have been disused, dismantled and built up, as was No. 39*a*. In addition, the Wall had been destroyed and rebuilt for at least 750 yards, with its thickness reduced by nearly eighteen inches and its new south face carried across the built-up recess of the turret. Such rebuilding of

PEEL CRAG, LOOKING WESTWARDS TO WINSHIELDS.

the Wall has already been noted at Throckley, Matfen Piers, Portgate, Planetrees and on the crags elsewhere.

The Wall now runs along a ridge of sandstone. It is at first in bad condition, but the ditch, with upcast-mound to north, is boldly developed. The crags shortly commence again, and the ditch ceases, in unfinished state. Before reaching the top of Winshields, and where the ditch ends, is milecastle 40 (Winshields), excavated in 1908. Its dimensions are similar to those of Castle Nick, and it also has gateways of small stones, no doubt because of the same difficulty of access. Its walls are uniformly six feet nine inches thick. The distances between milecastles 39, 40 and 41 are exceptionally long, measuring 1,806 and 1,850 yards respectively. Winshields stands 1,230 feet above sea level and is the highest point on the Wall: on a clear day the Solway is easily seen, with Burnswark in Dumfriesshire and Criffell in Kirkcudbright-shire forming a noble background.

The Wall, in good preservation, is here under guardianship of the Ministry of Public Building and Works, who have grouted the core afresh and reset the facing-stones. About 220 yards west of the summit of Winshields and eighty yards south of the Wall, in a sheltered spot called Green Slack, MacLauchlan observed British hut-circles. Turret 40a, 624 yards beyond the milecastle, has narrow walls and door to east. Next comes the deep valley of Lodham Slack, where the Wall, standing upon the Broad Foundation, has its ditch again, while to south MacLauchlan observed a native earthwork. Turret 40b, with narrow walls, is on the summit of the next ridge, and a gentle descent leads to milecastle 41 (Melkridge), a short-axis milecastle with narrow side-walls, examined in 1946.

The next gap, a bold one, is named Bogle Hole, and then comes Caw Gap. The way in which the Romans defended a re-entrant is well shown here. The Wall bends to south on each side of the gap, so as to enfilade any attack. The ditch is discontinued on the west side as soon as the crag attains height, but when the ground drops again for a few yards, opposite turret 41a, it reappears. A road passes

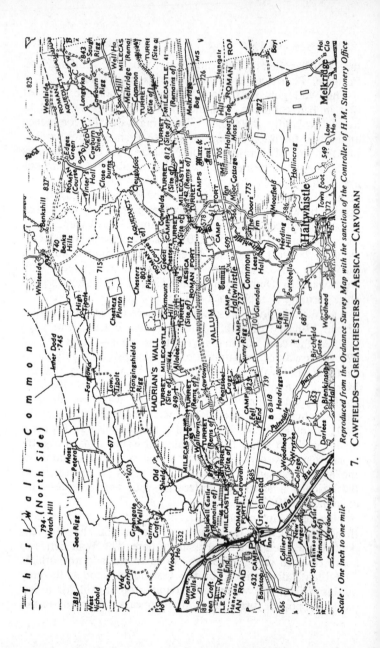

Scale : One inch to one mile

Reproduced from the Ordnance Survey Map with the sanction of the Controller of H.M. Stationery Office

7.   CAWFIELDS—GREATCHESTERS—AESICA—CARVORAN

through Caw Gap, and to north lies the solitary house of Burn Deviot, a resort of smugglers and sheep-stealers. Lights are believed to flicker at night about the windows, spirits of those murdered in the house.

West of Caw Gap, the Wall is largely uprooted for some distance. To the south two large stones, overlooking the Carlisle road, are called " The Mare and Foal" and one more is marked on Armstrong's *Map of Northumberland:* the three are probably remains of a Bronze-Age circle.

Proceeding onwards there is a point where the Wall is reduced in thickness by one foot at a single inset. The cliffs are again high and in columnar formation. After Bloody Gap and a second gap called Thorny Doors, comes turret 41*b*, with the Wall once more in excellent state. Here was found, fallen from the cliff, a building-stone, like a centurial stone, commemorating work by the Durotriges of Dorset through one of their tribal sub-divisions. It is matched by a duplicate from the same area and compares with similar tribal build-ing-stones from Thirlwall and Howgill.

On the east side of the next gap, named Hole Gap, is milecastle 42 (Cawfields), excavated by Clayton in 1848, at 1,641 yards west of milecastle 41. It measures internally sixty-three feet from east to west and forty-nine from north to south. Its walls stand seven or eight courses high and are eight feet thick. Both gates are of type I, in massive masonry, and the south gate displays a bar-hole for the doors. Excavation in 1936 showed that the north gate and wall were built to the Broad gauge, before the rest of the milecastle. Clayton's excavations produced two inscribed stones. The more important is a fragmentary inscription of Hadrian, matching those found at milecastles 37 and 38. The other is a tomb-stone, cut down to serve as a hearth-stone, and what remains of the inscription has been translated as " To the divine shades: Dagvalda, a soldier of (such and such a unit of) Pannonians lived . . . years; Pusinna erected this tablet ". South of the milecastle, on the Roman military way, three milestones have also been found; one of Severus Alexander (A.D. 222-23), the other of Numerian (A.D. 283-4), while the third, uninscribed, still lies on the spot. North of the Vallum and close to a vanished spring, was found an altar to Apollo. All five inscriptions are now in Chesters Museum. In Hole Gap is a short length of ditch, but from the adjacent summit to Haltwhistle Burn the Wall has been destroyed by Cawfields Quarry, now happily bought out by the nation. Here and at Carvoran the visitor may form a clear idea of what can happen to the noblest Roman monument in Britain, in

RE-USED TOMBSTONE, AND FRAGMENT OF HADRIANIC DEDICATION-SLAB, MILECASTLE 42 (CAWFIELDS), IN CHESTERS MUSEUM.

the noblest part of its course, at the remorseless hand of industry.

In this sector the Vallum, descending from Shield-on-the-Wall farm to Haltwhistle Burn, is in a perfection hardly equalled in any other part of its course. Excavation in 1939 revealed that, in the low wet ground between the track to the milecastle and the road to the quarry, the sides of its ditch had been revetted in turf-work, capped with clay and founded upon flagging. Uphill to east, the ditch has later been cleaned out and the marginal mound is present, while the crossings are absent. The gaps for the crossings, however, are clear in the north mound throughout the sector, with three long intervals at the east end; but in the south mound only three complete gaps have been dug, immediately west of Shield-on-the-Wall. Then comes a series of gaps only marked out, by a couple of V-shaped notches in the crest of the mound; next a length where not even that has been done; and then, half-way down the hill, the completed gaps begin again. Here, as at Wallend Common (p. 155) and High House (p. 175), the crossing-system was never completely finished.

The planning of the Military Way is also interesting. Opposite milecastle 42 it crosses the north mound of the Vallum, travels for 250 yards along the north berm and then recrosses the mound. The position of the Vallum in relation to the steep hill left no room for the road; but if the road had been contemplated when the Vallum was laid out, nothing would have been easier than to place the Vallum a little more to the south. The road is thus demonstrably later in the frontier-scheme than either Wall or Vallum.

The Stanegate, crossing the Carlisle road obliquely at the lane leading to Shield-on-the-Wall, aims for the Mare and Foal, but then curves off to south and runs parallel to the modern road. Where it approaches Haltwhistle Burn, a small fort stands sixty-five feet above the stream on a very bold bluff. The Stanegate swings round it to south, descends to the burn on a well-graded embankment and climbs the opposite bank by a deep cutting.

The fort, excavated in 1908, is 208 feet long by 167 feet wide, with an area of three-quarters of an acre; it is surrounded by deep ditches of irregular plan, and its ramparts were of earth with stone facing, set not in mortar but in clay. It had three gates, the west one a postern finally blocked. There were stone buildings inside it, comprising a barrack for a *centuria* (II, III) a granary (IV) and two rectangular structures (I, VI), perhaps offices. The pottery proved an occupation contemporary with the erection of the Wall; and it is significant that the fort had soon been carefully demolished, no doubt when the forts were moved forward to the line of the Wall itself. The demolished west rampart was buried beneath the refuse of a quarry, on whose rock-face

Clayton noted in 1844 the letters LEG. VI. V., a record of the Sixth Legion cutting stone, presumably for the Wall. This fort, in short, belongs to the initial design of the Wall.

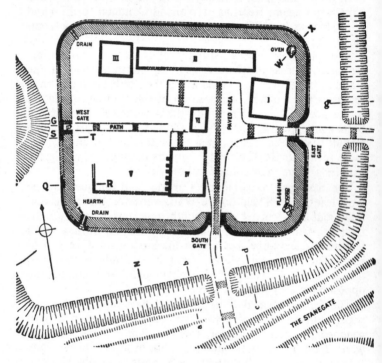

HALTWHISTLE BURN FORT.

Near the fort there is a remarkable group of temporary camps, some traceable with the aid of the Ordnance Map of Hadrian's Wall. Two lie to north; another 500 yards to east, and yet another double one 500 yards to west. A large and a small one lie north of the Wall; and along the Stanegate three more, one very small, a mile and more to the west and,

finally, a large one on Fell End. They cannot all well be of
the same date; and it has been suggested that some housed
men building the Wall, while others were constructed and
modified for training or exercise.

On the Haltwhistle Burn, the Cawfields quarry-spoil has
buried the site of a Roman water-mill, just below the point
where the burn is crossed by the Military Way. When the
structure was excavated, in 1908, part of the undershot
wooden mill-wheel was found; its large power-driven mill-
stones are in Chesters Museum.

West of Burnhead farm-house the Wall ditch is bold, but
the Wall is mostly destroyed. Turret 42*a* has been destroyed
by quarrying; 42*b* lies opposite the large temporary camp
beyond the Wall, close to the point where the Wall bends
westward towards Greatchesters.

FORT X   GREATCHESTERS (AESICA)

Greatchesters fort, like Carrawburgh, lies wholly south of
the Wall. It is nearly six miles from Housesteads, measures
419 by 355 feet over its rampart and covers just three acres.
Its function is to guard the Caw Gap. Like Housesteads, it
faces east; the Military Way enters by the *porta praetoria*
and leaves by the *porta decumana,* and a branch of the
Stanegate, on the site of the farm-road, comes in by the
porta principalis dextra.

The ancient name of the fort was AESICA, and its third-
century garrison, according to inscriptions, was the Second
cohort of Astures, with a detachment of Raeti Gaesati. The
Sixth cohort of Raeti and the Sixth cohort of Nervii, suc-
cessively, formed the later second century garrison, while
the *Notitia* mentions a First cohort of Astures, if this is
correct.

In Gordon's day some walls of this fort were standing
twelve or thirteen feet high. Today only rampart and ditch
are clearly defined, there being four ditches on the west side,
which is weakest.

Excavations in 1894 determined many features. The ramparts, as at several other Wall forts, were found to have had

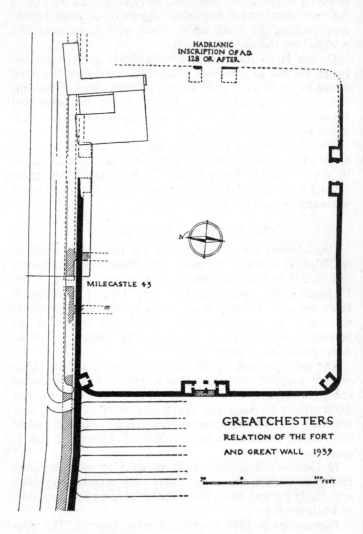

HADRIANIC
INSCRIPTION OF A.D.
128 OR AFTER

N

MILECASTLE 43

GREATCHESTERS
RELATION OF THE FORT
AND GREAT WALL 1939

50   0   100 FEET

lean-to buildings set against their inner face at a late date. The west tower of the south gate yielded a famous hoard of jewellery, comprising a brooch shaped as a hare, a gold brooch which is a masterpiece of Celtic art, a silver collar with pendant, a gold ring and a bronze ring with Gnostic gem. The west gate is of very special interest because it is the only gate on the Wall which still exhibits the blocking walls by which, after reconstruction of both portals under Severus, it was first reduced to one portal under Constantius and finally closed altogether; at other forts on the Wall such additions existed, but were cleared away by the excavators, usually without record. A large building inscription of Hadrian, mentioning his title of *Pater Patriae* conferred in 128, was found outside the east gate and is in Chesters Museum.

In view of this, the interesting part of the defences is the north-west angle, excavated in 1894 and 1925. The angle itself is rounded, but the angle-tower is planned with a projection and bonded with the Narrow Wall, thus clearly contemporary with the fort. The Narrow Wall, however, over-rides the butt-ends of the four west fort-ditches, which terminate behind the Broad Foundation, running in front of and parallel to it. The change from Broad Wall to Narrow Wall thus came when the ditches of the fort had already been dug, but before its rampart, which is of one build with the Narrow Wall, had been begun.

The reason why the Narrow Wall here was not built upon the Broad Foundation was discovered in 1939. Aesica occupies the site of milecastle 43, which had already been built, on the Broad Foundation, when the change to narrow gauge took place and the resolve to build a fort was made. The north gate of the milecastle could not be embodied in the defences of the fort, which were accordingly built just behind it, the milecastle being then demolished at leisure.

The headquarters building was partly uncovered in 1894, disclosing the cross-hall and administrative offices. Its vaulted underground strong-room, now ruinous, had been described by Lingard in 1807. It lay below the shrine of the standards, whence came an altar to Discipline also noted by Lingard. To north of the headquarters a granary produced a fine inscription, now at Newcastle, commemorating its rebuilding in A.D. 225. To south excavation disclosed the commandant's house, much rebuilt. Inscribed stones re-used in its walls included two tombstones and an ornate altar to Jupiter Dolichenus by a centurion of the Twentieth legion, Lucius Maximius Gaetulicus, who also saw service at Newstead on Tweed. South-west of this building are visible six rooms of a barrack, each built as a separate unit in the fourth-century manner seen at Housesteads.

To south and east of the fort is the *vicus*. The bath-house, discovered in 1897, lay 100 yards to south, east of the road to the Stanegate. Its features are clear from the plan: B is the dressing-room (*apodyterium*), E the latrine beside it; C the *frigidarium*, with cold bath D; A the *laconicum* of dry heat, G an ante-room. The large hall, H, beyond should be divided into two parts: first a square *tepidarium*, then a *caldarium* with apses for lavers and hot bath, next to the boiler and furnace. The final destruction of the *caldarium* was associated with a hoard of late third-century coins.

The Vallum passes to south of the fort and was crossed by an original revetted causeway, of which the east side was found in 1951. Further south are traces of barrows, where the cemetery of the fort seems to have been; but the " remarkable " barrows noted near the Wall by Brand would seem to have been prehistoric burials. Cultivation-terraces on the hillside west of the fort resemble those at Housesteads and are associated with medieval or later homesteads.

A remarkable feature of this fort is the aqueduct which feeds it from the north. Lingard noted that the " water for the station was brought by a winding aqueduct still visible from the head of Haltwhistle burn. It winds 5 miles ". This is a channel or leet, three or four feet deep and proportionately wide, running along the north margin of the basin of the Caw Burn; and, in order to cross its northern tributaries, a very winding course is taken, but the line is so well planned that only once has a bridge or embankment been necessary.

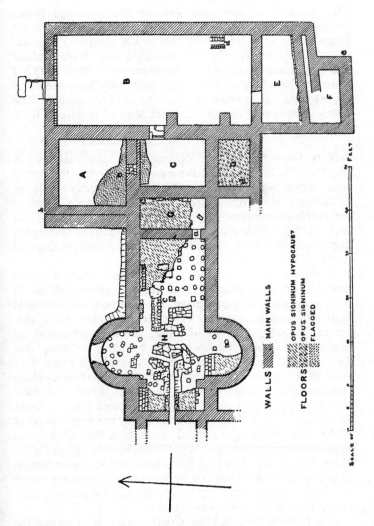

BATH-HOUSE AT AESICA.

This structure is now gone, but its site is named Benks Bridge. The aqueduct is in fact six miles long, though the direct line is little more than two and a quarter. The water from Caw Burn was so brought to within about three hundred and fifty yards of the fort. The aqueduct is then lost, but owing to the falling ground, water could only have been here conveyed by an embankment or an inverted siphon. The course is indicated on the Ordnance Map of Hadrian's Wall.

FROM GREATCHESTERS TO CARVORAN

Near Greatchesters the Vallum is of great interest. A quarter of a mile west of the causeway serving the fort it runs almost straight, into a large field directly south of Cockmount Hill farm house. Here ten successive crossings are visible in complete state, with causeways in the ditch and gaps in both mounds, though a modern track somewhat obscures those in the south mound, while a modern drain in the ditch has slightly disturbed the causeways. Excavation in 1939 showed that the causeways were made when the ditch had been open sufficiently long for the upper half of its very steep sides to wash down into the bottom. Vegetable matter then grew, and next came the causeways. These preserved, behind their mass of filling, the steep profile of the original ditch, here modified only by the weathering that had occurred before the causeways were placed there. This state of affairs is exceedingly rare: for almost everywhere else the Vallum ditch has been re-cut, as in the next field, where upcast from later clearing can be seen piled in heaps on the lip. The Vallum then runs along the north slope of Blake Law, avoiding the marsh at its foot. The ditch is cut into the slope for 250 yards and for the western 100 yards the slope is stepped to form the south berm and the south mound is unusually broad. Then the Vallum swings across the marsh and runs along its north margin. In the Allolee grounds cultivation has reduced it to poor condition.

The Narrow Wall, leaving Greatchesters, runs behind the Broad Foundation up to turret 43a, which had already been built upon the latter. Broad foundation and Narrow Wall then run parallel again as far as Cockmount Hill Wood, where both are exposed to view, but before leaving the wood the two gradually converge, so that the Narrow Wall runs on the Broad foundation as usual. The reason for their long divergence is probably due to insistence by the engineers of the Narrow Wall upon laying a deeper foundation, though they were normally content to use the shallow broad one. From Aesica to Allolee the Military Way is very plain, and

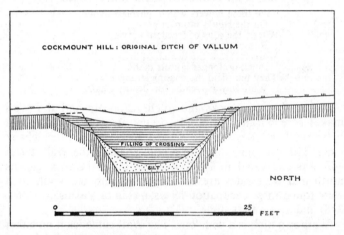

COCKMOUNT HILL: ORIGINAL DITCH OF VALLUM

FILLING OF CROSSING

SILT

NORTH

0   25   FEET

THE VALLUM DITCH, IN ORIGINAL FORM.

one of its uninscribed milestones forms the west post of the gate at the west end of Cockmount Hill Wood, on the Wall-line. The Wall now climbs gradually. Turret 43*b* is a hundred yards beyond the edge of the wood. The ditch becomes irregular, dug now fully and now to half width, but often not at all. Here and there the north face of the Wall is seen in short lengths.

East of Allolee farm house, the site of the long-axis mile-castle 44 (Allolee) is very distinct. Beyond it the rebuilt north face of the Wall stands up to nine courses high for about 200 yards. Opposite Allolee farm house only the core is seen. Of two centurial stones recorded in the south wall of the farm house, one is lost and the other very indistinct. Beyond milecastle 44 the crags are broken by frequent gaps, known as the " Nine Nicks of Thirlwall ". The Wall climbs and descends them unflinchingly, seizing the crest of the rugged cliff, wherever possible.

Sir Walter Scott knew this part of the Wall, which evoked a gallant poem from his pen:

To a Lady, With Flowers from a Roman Wall, 1797

Take these flowers which, purple waving,
　　On the ruin'd rampart grew,
Where, the sons of freedom braving,
　　Rome's imperial standards flew.
Warriors from the breach of danger
　　Pluck no longer laurels there;
They but yield the passing stranger
　　Wild-flower wreaths for Beauty's hair.

In the first two nicks the ditch reappears and the Wall makes a re-entrant; turret 44*a* occurs at a turn on the crest between them. Beyond the second nick comes Mucklebank Crag, 860 feet high, where in a bold angle of the Wall, turret 44*b* was excavated in 1892. Because it lies in an angle, its north and west sides are both recessed into the Wall. In it were found three occupation-levels, a coin of Valens (A.D. 364-378) and a centurial stone.

Walltown nick is a wide one. The Wall enfilades it on either side and runs across it in a straight line, accompanied by the ditch. Close behind the Wall, in the middle of the gap, is a spring, now enclosed in a shaft, called " The King's Well " or " King Arthur's Well ". Hutchinson records a tradition that here Paulinus baptised King Egbert, and himself suggested King Edwin; but neither notion is true. Camden learnt of a more picturesque tradition, connected with chives, which still grow abundantly in the crevices of the crags near Walltown House. " That the Roman souldiers of the marches did plant heere every where in old time for their use, certaine medicin- able hearbs, for to cure wounds: whence is it that some Emperick practitioners of Chirurgery in Scotland, flock hither every yeere in the beginning of summer, to gather such simples and wound herbes; the vertue whereof they highly commend as found by long experience, and to be of singular efficacy ". In fact this plant (*Lilium schoenoprasum*), though rare, frequents rocky pastures in widely distributed parts of Britain. The suggestion that Romans introduced it is not impossible, but not proven.

Walltown is also the site of the tower inherited by John Ridley, brother of the Protestant martyr. The present Walltown farm-house is modern, but a fragment of the tower remained in Wallis's time and MacLauchlan saw its foundations to north-west of the present house. These have now vanished, as has the old village of Walltown on the south slope nearby. To east of Walltown farm a small hill carried a British entrenchment.

After climbing the steep west side of Walltown Nick, the Wall, of which much core is visible, runs along the crag to milecastle 45 (Walltown). This is a long-axis milecastle, and large stones robbed from its gateway lie behind troughs east of Walltown farm. A fine piece of the Wall runs to the edge of the Greenhead Quarry, 150 yards away. This extension of the quarry has removed the Wall for a quarter of a mile. Beyond it turret 45*a* and some 400 yards of Wall are under guardianship of the Ministry of Public Building and Works, and rank among the finest stretches of the Wall, especially in the fifth nick, beyond the turret. This turret is especially remarkable, for it was built as an isolated tower before the Wall was brought up to its east and west sides and its foundations, examined in 1959, produced early Hadrianic and slightly earlier potsherds; the only other example of the kind is Pike Hill tower (p. 177). Both are situated on prominent points for signalling and are long-distance signal-towers independent of the milecastle and turret system. This one lies almost 100 yards short of the normal measured position, if it served as a true turret. The western bite of the Greenhead Quarry has then removed the rest of the Nine Nicks and the Wall with them, including turret 45*b*, one of the most savage and deplorable incursions of industry upon the Wall.

The Wall and Vallum now converge upon Carvoran. The Stanegate, which has been running along the ridge behind both to Fell End, where it passes through a large marching-camp, crosses the flats towards the fort. Near here was found, in 1932, a milestone of Aurelian (A.D. 270-275), very like that of Probus (A.D. 276-282) found at Crindledykes, seven Roman miles further east of the same road.

FORT XI   CARVORAN (MAGNA)

Carvoran is the MAGNA of the *Notitia,* which records its garrison as the second cohort of Dalmatae, also attested by a tombstone. In Hadrian's day it was held by the first cohort of Hamian archers, a special Syrian unit, whose native weapon was the bow; and their commander, under whom the fort-wall was built, set up an altar for the health of Aelius Caesar, in A.D. 136-138. The same unit was again in garrison under Calpurnius Agricola in A.D. 162, when it set up altars, now at Newcastle and at Chesters.

The site lies at the junction of the Stanegate and the Maiden Way, which, passing the fort of Whitley Castle near Alston, crossed the north shoulder of Cross Fell and joined the York-Carlisle road at Kirkby Thore. Its purpose was primarily to guard the road-junction, and this may have been the task of a pre-Hadrianic fort in this position, though no such fort has yet been disclosed. It also overlooks the important gap of the Tipalt valley, which its archer-garrison was very well fitted to command. The connexion of the fort with the Stanegate rather than the Wall is supported by the deliberate exclusion of the site from the military zone of the Wall by the Vallum, which runs to north of it and there avoids a deep marsh by a northward deviation. A secondary crossing in this deviation carried a roadway from the fort's north gate.

The fort measured some 440 by 360 feet over the ramparts, enclosing about $3\frac{1}{2}$ acres, as at Chesterholm and Castlesteads. Centurial stones show that it was walled in stone by the Hamians late in Hadrian's reign. The north-west angle-tower is visible, but little is known of internal buildings. In 1599 Camden found the ruins " very evident ", but agriculture had begun to destroy them by 1776 and the process was completed in 1837. The only building then observed was a bath-house with plastered walls, situated, as at Risingham or Bewcastle, just within the south wall and near the southwest angle of the fort. Its dressing-room contained the altar for the health of Aelius Caesar already noted.

Knowledge of Carvoran thus depends largely upon relics. The most important building-stones are an inscription of Hadrian, not more specifically to be dated, and the inscriptions from the fort-wall, of not long before A.D. 135-8, when

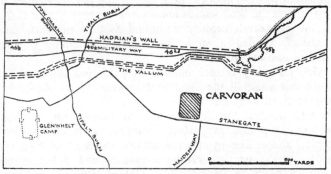

THE WALL, VALLUM, FORT AND STANEGATE, AT CARVORAN.

the Hamian cohort was in garrison. The deities who came with them are represented by dedications to the goddesses Syria and Hammia. There is a very remarkable metrical dedication to the Virgin of the Zodiac, with reference to Julia Domna, by a prefect honoured with tribune's rank. More usual are the dedications, to Fortune, by a centurion who had served in all three British legions, and to the Nymphs, by some female settlers. A small altar to Epona, the ostlers' goddess, smacks of the fort stabling. A well within the fort yielded fine stag's antlers, eloquent of hunting prospects, and a perfect iron javelin-head, now in the Museum of Antiquities at Newcastle, with a double barb on a long stem, socketed for a wooden shaft. The weapon is of the kind used in the later Roman period by German tribes.

The extra-mural settlement is represented by many dedications to the god Vitiris, whose altars are confined to the Wall and its neighbourhood and centre upon Carvoran, as if the cult had its seat hereabouts. He is equated with the Roman Hercules and also with the Celtic god Mogon; and, by confusion of *Vitiris* with the Latin *veteres*, sometimes gets a ghost plural as *di veteres*. This deity seems to have been German but an undoubted north-British deity, Belatucadrus, is named on a Carvoran altar.

The cemetery has produced tombstones, notably that of a soldier in the Twentieth legion, one of the few legionaries in garrison on the Wall who is known to have been buried there. In the eighteenth century a mound east of the fort, now vanished, yielded a stone coffin case containing organic remains and two gold rings.

One discovery is rare indeed. In 1915, just north of the north-east angle of the fort, what looked like an old bucket was seen sticking out of the ground. This proved to be a Roman *modius,* or dry-measure, in bronze. Of excellent workmanship and in perfect condition, it is of truncated conical shape, like an inverted bucket, about a foot high and wide, weighs nearly twenty-six pounds and holds twenty pints. It bears an inscription in elegant lettering, certifying its weight and capacity and once naming the Emperor Domitian, under whom it was made; the name, however, has been erased following the condemnation of his memory by the Senate. The measure is stated to hold $17\frac{1}{2}$ *sextarii,* now 16·8 pints, but will hold almost twenty. It has been suggested that this was a device to defraud provincials under obligation to deliver a certain amount of wheat; but Roman certified measures are normally quite accurate, and a gauge set lower than the brim may be missing, since there are rivet-holes for vanished accessories. This most unusual object is one of the notable exhibits in Chesters Museum.

FROM CARVORAN TO BIRDOSWALD

The site of milecastle 46 (Carvoran) lies just west of the northward deviation of the Vallum, mentioned above. Here, and down the hill as far as Thirlwall Castle, the Wall ditch is particularly striking; while the lines of the Vallum, running parallel with the Wall, are also clear almost as far as the river Tipalt. In an outhouse at Holmhead a Roman inscribed stone is inserted, upside down, and reads CIVITAS DVMNONI(*orum*), in a latish style of lettering. The Dumnonii were the British tribe occupying Devonshire, Cornwall, and part of Somersetshire. This stone would seem to record work on the Wall by their levies; similar stones record work in other sectors by the Catuvellauni of Hertfordshire and the Durotriges of Dorset. They constitute a highly instructive exception to the rule that the Wall was, in the main, built by military labour. On this occasion at least the tribal levy, or *corvée* was called into service, but for repairs rather than original building.

The Stanegate zig-zags up the hill to north of Greenhead. As the slope evens out towards the crest Glenwhelt Leazes camp is seen to south; it measures some 495 by 264 feet over the ramparts and its gates,

BUILDING-STONE OF A BRITISH TRIBAL *corvée*, HOLMHEAD.

of rare type, have an external traverse combined with an internal *clavicula* or hooked termination of the rampart. Another smaller camp of the same type lies at Chapel Rigg, over half a mile west-south-west of this one; and a third, with ordinary traverse gateways, at Crooks, a mile and a quarter due west. All are temporary works, similar in construction and purpose to those near Haltwhistle Burn.

The Wall and Vallum reappear on the slope west of the road and railway. West of the road the Broad Foundation stood three courses high and the ditch was about 33 feet wide and 6 feet deep. Between Wallend and Chapel House, the ditch of the Wall is unusually large. Its north side, or counterscarp, is fifteen or even twenty feet high. Towards the west end of Wallend Common the Vallum is notable. Gaps for the crossings have been dug in both mounds, yet the material has never been used to make the causeways, but lies untidily outside the gaps in small heaps as it was dumped from baskets by the diggers. The crossing system has evidently never been completed, as at Shield-on-the-Wall and High House.

Three hundred yards east of Chapel House comes milecastle 47 (Chapelhouse), excavated in 1935, and measuring internally 69 feet from north to south and some 60 feet from east to west. Its gateways were of type II, and, as at milecastle 48 (Poltross Burn), a large barracks lay on each side of the roadway. Its original dedication-tablet, once built up

PART OF A HADRIANIC DEDICATION-SLAB FROM MILECASTLE 47
(CHAPEL HOUSE), AT NEWCASTLE.

in a stable at Chapel House, was set up by the Twentieth legion, and differs in style from the Second legion's tablets. Turret 47a stood at the normal interval westwards. At the hamlet of Gap, on the watershed between Tyne and Irthing, the Vallum, here very distinct, takes higher ground than the Wall. In the gable end and in the lowest course but one, at the angle of an out-house, a centurial stone is seen, upside down: it reads, translated, " The century of Claudius Augustanus, of the third cohort ". Just beyond the hamlet is the site of turret 47b.

The ditch of the Wall between Gap and the railway at Gilsland is unusually large, measuring fifty feet wide in several places. On a knoll called Rose Hill, later removed in making Gilsland railway station, Lingard observed " a platform on the top twelve yards in diameter, with a ditch round it. Here was a figure of flying Victory ". His description of the hill strongly suggests a medieval motte: and builders of such castles elsewhere took packing-stones for their wooden structures from Roman sites. The stone, much weathered but of particular interest for its representation of a domed shrine comparable with Arthur's O'on, near Falkirk, is now at Rockcliffe, north of Carlisle.

Immediately west of the railway station the wooded gorge of Poltross Burn divides Northumberland and Cumberland. The Vallum, here under guardianship of the Ministry of Public Building and Works, approached the stream by deep

F·W·FAIRHOLT.

SCULPTURED FRAGMENT FROM ROSE HILL, GILSLAND,
AT ROCKCLIFFE, CUMBERLAND.

cuttings through each bank, the steep sides of its ditch revetted with masonry. The Military Way, swerving southward to ease the gradient, crosses the burn between the Vallum and the Wall and avoids milecastle 48 (Poltross Burn), on the west bank of the burn, by breaching the north mound of the Vallum and running along the north berm, where it remains for at least 600 yards.

The milecastle is also under guardianship of the Ministry (plan, p. 20) and measures internally seventy feet from north to south and sixty feet nine inches from east to west. All its walls were built to the Broad gauge, the Narrow Wall on Broad foundation joining wing-walls about twelve feet away from the milecastle on either side. The north gate, 9½ feet

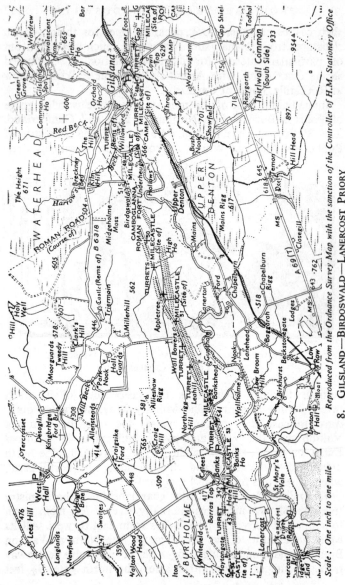

Reproduced from the Ordnance Survey Map with the sanction of the Controller of H.M. Stationery Office

8. GILSLAND—BIRDOSWALD—LANERCOST PRIORY

Scale : One inch to one mile

wide and of type III, had secondary pivot-blocks and was reduced in the Severan reconstruction to a four-foot postern. Enough remained of a flight of steps leading to the rampart-walk at the north-east corner to show by calculation, that the rampart-walk lay twelve feet above ground, which, allowing for the steep hillside, suggests fifteen Roman feet as the external height of the Wall without its parapet. Two barrack-buildings flanked the axial street, and a series of ovens occupied the north-west corner. No inscription was discovered, but finds prove an occupation from early in the reign of Hadrian to the late fourth century, with reconstructions in A.D. 197, 297 and 369. At this milecastle type B construction, as west of milecastle 17, is again seen in the Wall foundation, comprising three courses of stonework above the flag founda-tion, followed by an offset marking the commencement of the superstructure; and this continues to Willowford Bridge.

The Stanegate, after running almost straight from Green-head towards milecastle 48, curves to south and crosses Poltross Burn 350 yards upstream from the Wall. Two hun-dred yards west of this crossing, on the crest of the ridge north-east of Throp farm, stood a small Roman fort, excavated in 1910 and resembling in size and date the fort at Haltwhistle Burn. About 200 feet square, it covers seven-eighths of an acre including the rampart, which was of turf on a stone foundation. Its two gateways were of timber and so had doubtless been the internal buildings, while the pottery showed an occupation contemporary with the building of the Wall, followed by a second brief use in the fourth century. The Stanegate, passing to north, continues south-west to Mains Rigg signal-tower and the fort at Nether Denton.

The Wall crosses the railway immediately beyond mile-castle 48, and stands several courses high in the old Vicarage garden, east of Gilsland School, now belonging to Romanway Guest House, where it is again under Ministry guardianship. This is a good place to study the Broad foundation in relation to the Narrow Wall. The flag footing-course of the Broad Wall, visible at the bottom of the garden, carries one course of Wall-stones; a little way up the slope a second course is seen, and then a third. But no appreciable time can have elapsed between laying these lower courses of the Broad Wall and building the Narrow Wall upon them, for the mortar core of the two is homogeneous and continuous. Here was found a centurial stone, inscribed COH I > OPSILI, " The first cohort, century of Opsilius:" there are also two Roman altars, once built into the sanctuary steps of the Norman church at Over Denton; one uninscribed, the other dedicated by a tribune to Jupiter, Best and Greatest and worn by use as a threshold or by sharpening implements or weapons.

Across the Brampton road Wall and Vallum converge until the north mound of the Vallum comes within some fifteen feet of the Wall. A fine stretch of the Wall is here seen, as Narrow Wall on Broad foundation. In it were found four centurial stones, two reading COH VI > LOVSI SVAVIS, two of >COCCEI REGVLI, both known in other sectors, the former thrice. On Willowford Hill, to south, there is a well-preserved temporary camp with two gates protected by traverses, in contiguous sides. It is one and a quarter acres in size.

The Wall is now preserved and displayed by the Ministry as far as Willowford, and just east of the point where river, Wall and Vallum are closest comes turret 48a, with well-preserved wing-walls of the Broad gauge. Two hundred yards farther on, the farm-track crosses the Wall and occupies the ditch, here enhanced by the cart-track which occupies it. The remains of turret 48b stand high and bold just before reaching the farm-yard.

The Wall then descends to flat ground bordering the river, and reaches the bridge by which it crossed the Irthing. On the east, the first feature is a large tower, founded upon massive re-used masonry and built against the back of the Narrow Wall, here resting upon the four courses of Broad foundation. The west wall of this tower coincides with the end of the east wing-wall of an original turret. Only the north-east corner of the recess of this turret, however, now remains, all else having been removed in a drastic Roman reconstruction. The turret guarded the abutment of the original bridge, now seen as a splayed foundation slightly further west. The reconstructed Wall rides across this earliest abutment and terminates over a pair of narrow culverts of large masonry, probably serving a mill. The front of this Wall was once faced in large blocks, now mostly replaced by a patched face; and these bonded with a massive stone apron, revetting the end of the berm as it approached the river. The north front of the apron is cut to match the slope of the ditch, and there are traces of paving in the adjacent river-channel. Next, the

EAST END OF ROMAN BRIDGE, WILLOWFORD

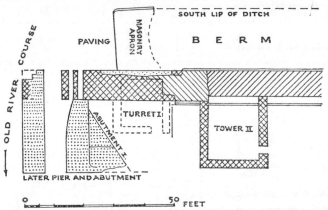

early splayed abutment was enlarged, by blocking the east culvert, while a correspondingly large pier was added in the stream, forming a new culvert with paved bottom to serve as the race for an undershot water-mill wheel. A stone spindle-bearing, belonging either to the wheel or to the power-driven mill-stones, was found on the enlarged abutment. Both enlargement and water-mill are matched at the North Tyne, where a bridge sufficiently wide to carry the Military Way replaced the narrow first bridge and a mill-race is associated with the later work.

The main water-piers of the bridge are represented only by the large pier already described, which incorporates work of

the first period at its north end. It also embodied re-used
masonry, including a voussoir, while two haunch-stones from
a massive segmental arch appear in the south foundations of
the late tower (Tower II on plan); as if the early bridge, as
at Chesters, had carried the Wall itself across the river.
Excavation in 1940 showed that the river once flowed immediately west of the abutment in a rocky gorge, which contained
foundations of two further water-piers, now ten feet below

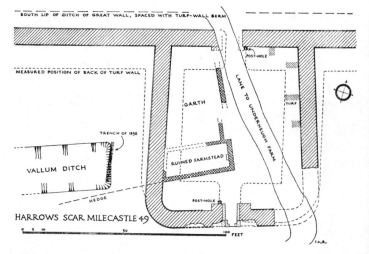

the surface of the holm. The turbulent Irthing has evidently
changed its course since Roman times, so that it now lies west
of the entire Roman bridge. This means that the western
cliff of Harrow's Scar may then have been considerably less
steep and thus easier for the Wall to climb.

On the cliff summit the Wall stands seven courses high and
joins milecastle 49 (Harrow's Scar), found in 1898 to measure
internally seventy-five feet long from north to south by sixty-
five feet wide from east to west. In 1953 further excavation
revealed part of the Turf-Wall milecastle below it, and showed
that the Vallum ditch, ending just short of its southwest
corner, did not descend the cliff. The south gate of the stone

milecastle was of type III, reduced in the third century to a foot-way.

At the Irthing the Broad Wall came to an end and its counterpart, the Turf Wall, began. When the latter was replaced in stone, the new Stone Wall was the Narrow Wall, and this, between Harrow's Scar and a point west of Birdoswald, is conserved by the Ministry of Public Building and Works and forms a fine sight. At about fifty yards west of the milecastle it makes a northward turn of about eight degrees: had it not done so, it would have aimed for the main east gate of Birdoswald fort.

FORT XII   BIRDOSWALD (CAMBOGLANNA)

Birdoswald fort is nearly three miles and a quarter from Carvoran. Its position is striking. In addition to the bold scarp on the south, at the foot of which winds the Irthing, a valley to north carries eastward the overflow of Midgeholm Moss. The west side now appears weak, but was in Roman times a fairly deep bog, draining below the fort into the gully which emerges in the cliff west of Underheugh. The prime function of the fort, however, was to guard the Irthing bridge and to watch the route from the north across the shoulder of Gillalees Beacon.

The fort is named AMBOGLANNA in the *Notitia,* but the Rudge Cup and Amiens skillet show that this was an error for CAMBOGLANNA, which has the very suitable meaning " Crook Bank ". The garrison in the fourth century was the First cohort of Dacians and in the third the First cohort of Thracians as well. The fort measures 580 by 400 feet, and has an area of five acres and a third. Like Benwell, Rudchester, Halton-chesters and Chesters, it has four main gates and two posterns, one at each end of the via quintana.

ALTAR FROM
BIRDOSWALD, BY
THE FIRST COHORT
OF DACIANS
(TULLIE HOUSE).

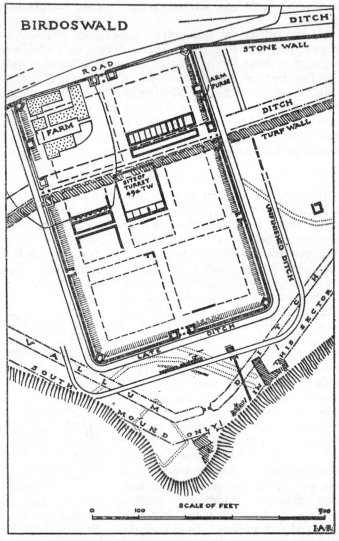

BIRDOSWALD FORT. WITH TURF WALL, VALLUM, AND STONE WALL.

The north gate lies under the modern road, where the foundations of one of its jambs used to be seen in the metal-ling. The curved north-west angle of the fort, twelve courses high, forms the east side of the drive entrance to Birdoswald Farm, and the Wall abutted upon it with little attempt at bonding. The Wall had been rebuilt in the late fourth century over a ditch, as if the fort had been cut off from the Wall for independent defence during a crisis, as Kipling fancied in *Puck of Pook's Hill*. The well preserved angle-tower was used as a cook-house, its ovens often rebuilt during the second century. The fort-wall then continues southwards and exhibits an interval-tower standing high except at the robbed front. The shrubbery in the farm-house garden covers the main west gate. The west postern has wheel-ruts in its threshold and pivot-holes for a two-leaved door. It was blocked during the Roman period, probably under Severus, whose internal build-ings straddled the street which it served.

At the south-west angle the rampart, though not high, bears marks of very thorough reconstruction; two successive periods of Roman work can be traced, and a third is to be associated with a long-vanished farm-building.

The south gate, cleared in 1851, is the usual twin entrance. The east portal was blocked soon after erection and converted into a guard-room. Late in the Roman period, the west portal was also closed. The blocking walls were removed in 1851, but the east guardchamber has not been excavated, unlike the other, which has since become choked by its own ruins. The east wall of the west guardchamber is reconstructed in large and irregular masonry following complete demolition, in the style of the late fourth century. To west of the guardchamber there is a corn-drying kiln of post-Roman date.

Both gates on the east side of the fort have been excavated, and the blocked postern is now to be seen. In the late fourth century the fort wall was entirely rebuilt here, on the crest of the bank, after having already been reconstructed in large masonry in the third century. The rampart backing, between the south-east angle and the postern, was cut back to form a flat revetted shelf used for cooking-ovens in the early fourth-century, while the rampart-walk had a vertical back. The main east gate, in excellent preservation, was excavated in 1852, when many traces of the alterations which it had undergone were removed. Its north portal and tower are founded in the Turf-Wall ditch. The north portal was later blocked, but not until after the central pier had been strengthened and a

THE RIGHT-HAND MEMBER OF A PAIR OF BUILDING-STONES FROM THE EAST GATE, BIRDOSWALD (NEWCASTLE).

Severan roadway and new pivot-stones had been provided. When blocked, the portal became a guard-room, of which the back wall still stands, the front one having been removed in 1852. The Romans also blocked the west door of the original guardchamber and opened a new door in its south wall, giving access from the new guard-room built in the portal. At this time the south guardchamber may have received a hypocaust.

Fallen masonry found in 1852 outside the south tower included a re-used inscription, which may be translated: "Under Modius Julius, Imperial propraetorian legate, the First Aelian cohort of Dacians, commanded by Marcus Claudius Menander, tribune." Modius Julius was governor in

A.D. 219, and the stone was doubtless matched by another bearing the name and titles of Elagabalus, under whom the work was done. To left of the inscription is the palm-branch of victory, to right the curved native sword of the Dacians. Several round-headed lintels for doors or windows come from near this and other gates, as at Housesteads; one was placed over the door of the north guardchamber in 1852, but incorrectly. To north of the gate a fine stretch of fort-wall and an interval-tower are seen. Between tower and gate a bronze arm-purse, like that from Barcombe (p. 34) was found in 1949. It contained 28 *denarii* current under Hadrian and had been accidentally buried when the rampart-backing was piled against the fort-wall, behind which the purse had been momentarily laid aside.

The whole interior was once marked with the line of streets and the ruins of buildings. Towards the rear of the fort the normal barracks have been found, and a coin-hoard of 30 *denarii*, again those current under Hadrian, was concealed in the primary floor of one of them. Later the buildings were drastically reconstructed and extended across the *via quintana*. Near the east postern, a building of three rooms, one heated by a hypocaust, was, to judge from similar buildings in other forts, the baths of the commandant's house. It yielded a fine seated statue of Fortune, identifiable by the tip of her rudder, now at Tullie House Museum, Carlisle.

West of this, in the centre of the fort, stood the headquarters building. Trial trenches in 1930 showed that, because the ground here dipped into a natural gully, the back wall of the building stands some 15 courses high, while the voussoirs of its arched front lie just as they have fallen. The front wall, on the other hand, is only two courses high.

West of the headquarters one or more granaries lay parallel with the main cross-street of the fort. In 1859, in making the garden in front of the farm house, the south wall of one of them was adapted as a retaining-wall. It has nine external buttresses, between each of which is a vertical slot ventilator. The buttresses supported the thrust of the heavy roof, and the air-vents ventilated the space beneath the damp-proof floor and kept it cool. Three sleeper walls, to support the flagged floor, were found to north and many roofing slabs lay among the fallen rubbish.

The *praetentura,* or area to north of the central buildings, contained barrack-blocks lying, as at Chesters, across the fort. Those immediately north of the *via principalis* overlie the filled-in ditch of the Turf Wall and one of them, excavated in 1928-9, produced inscriptions important for the history of the fort, described below. In the *retentura,* or rearward part of the fort, trenching has shown that under Severus buildings were laid across the *via quintana,* to house the extra troops then added to the garrison.

The relation of the Stone Wall, Turf Wall and Vallum to the fort is complicated and has given rise to much curious planning. The Stone Wall is brought up to the fort's north angles. The Turf Wall, running straight from milecastle 49, abutted upon its principal gates, like the Stone Wall at Chesters; but both the Turf Wall and its ditch were there first, for, in 1945 and 1894 respectively, they were found to pass below the fort. The site of turret 49*a* TW was also found in 1945, represented by a gap in the Turf Wall and a scatter of mason's chippings left from the removal of the tower, all sealed below the *via principalis* of the fort. The Vallum is diverted round the south side of the fort, only just slipping between it and the Irthing escarpment, at the cost of omitting the north mound. Opposite the south gate of the fort the Vallum was interrupted by a causeway of undisturbed subsoil, revetted vertically on each side with stone and closed by an undefended gate, as at Benwell. In fact, the first arrangement of the fort, in relation to Turf Wall and Vallum is normal.

Three points, however, differentiate Birdoswald from other sites. First, the Vallum cuts through an earlier native promontory-fort, itself occupied by a small Roman rectangular post associated with early second-century pottery. Secondly, the Vallum obliterated a series of temporary wooden buildings erected during the building of the fort and was later crossed by the first ditches cut round the fort. Thirdly, when the Stone Wall replaced the Turf Wall it was run up to the northern angles of the fort, probably to gain room for a parade ground and other buildings to the east; for to west the ground was boggy and undeveloped in Roman times.

The history of the fort and the Wall in general was illuminated by two large inscriptions, found in 1929 and now at Tullie House Museum, Carlisle. One records the restoration of a granary (*horreum*) by the First Dacian cohort and First cohort of Thracians, in A.D. 205-208; this marks the Severan rebuilding of the Wall after the disaster of 197. The other records the restoration of the *praetorium, principia* and a bath-house under Diocletian and his colleagues, after A.D. 297. These inscriptions gave the first definite dates for the commencement of the second and third periods of occupation long recognised as Wall sites. The second, which, in translation, describes the commandant's house as "fallen into ruin and covered with earth" is unique in its admission of the effects of devastation and abandonment.

Four objects of interest, visible from Birdoswald, may also be mentioned. In the valley, not half a mile due south is Over Denton church. Its chancel-arch, of the eleventh or twelfth century and six feet in span, is built of Roman arch-stones, whose original tooling was unfortunately removed by re-cutting in 1881.

A quarter of a mile south-west of the church, on the hillock of Mains Rigg, overlooking the railway-crossing, a Roman signal-tower was identified in 1928. It is a stone tower twenty-one feet square, girt by a ditch with causeway. Being isolated, it had no door on the ground-floor but must have been entered by a removable ladder. It links the Stanegate forts of Throp and Nether Denton, invisible from one another, and the Stanegate itself coincides with the modern road.

The third object, seen to north-west from the road north of the fort is a ruined wall of Triermain Castle, celebrated by Scott in *The Bridal of Triermain* and by Coleridge in *Christabel*. The fourth object lies near the summit of Gillalees Beacon, on the horizon a little west of north, and is seen as a small cairn-like mound in good weather. Named Robin Hood's Butt, it is a Roman signal-tower flanking the Roman

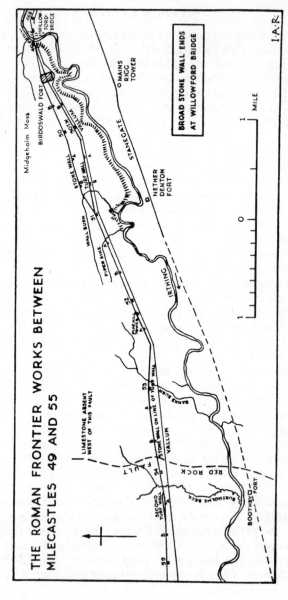

THE ROMAN FRONTIER WORKS BETWEEN MILECASTLES 49 AND 55

BROAD STONE WALL ENDS AT WILLOWFORD BRIDGE

I·A·R·

road from Birdoswald to Bewcastle, an outpost fort six miles to north-west. It is in all essentials like Mains Rigg, and signals from it could be seen at Birdoswald or on the Wall, but not by the enemy to north, so that a surprise intercepting move could be prepared in terrain well adapted to ambush.

FROM BIRDOSWALD TO CASTLESTEADS

The Wall westward from Birdoswald is the Narrow Wall, on a foundation less deep than that between Wallsend and Newcastle. Its remains are on the south side of the road, and have been preserved by the Ministry to beyond turret 49*b*, excavated in 1911. A little more than half a mile from the

FRAGMENT OF HADRIANIC BUILDING-INSCRIPTION IN OAK, FROM
TURF-WALL MILECASTLE 50 TW (TULLIE HOUSE).

fort, on the crest, is the site of milecastle 50 (High House), also excavated in 1911 and found to measure internally seventy-six feet from north to south and sixty from east to west. It resembles milecastles 48 and 49 in plan and details, and its walls are narrow (seven feet seven inches) since it was built with the Narrow Wall.

The Turf Wall, running behind the line of the Stone Wall from milecastle 49 to milecastle 51, is first visible in the second field west of Birdoswald, behind turret 49*b*. Mound and ditch are here faint and have been washed out on the steep slope, but soon become bold and so continue to milecastle 51. When the Turf Wall was discovered, in 1895 (its ditch had been noted previously, though not understood), the view was advanced that Hadrian had constructed a Turf Wall from sea to sea, but that only this short piece remained, the rest having been dismantled when Severus built the Stone

Wall on the same line. It was argued that any Hadrianic remains associated with milecastles and turrets elsewhere could not disprove this, since they might have belonged to the supposed Turf Wall just as well as to the Stone Wall.

The question was settled by excavating Stone-Wall milecastle 50 and turrets 49*b*, 50*a* and 50*b;* for these occurred in the one and only sector where the Turf Wall and Stone Wall ran on different lines. Conclusive proof of Hadrianic occupation was found in them all. This showed that both the Stone Wall and the Turf Wall were the work of Hadrian. As for the original length of the Turf Wall, it was ascertained in 1927 that it did not extend east of the Irthing, where the Broad Stone Wall was in fact its counterpart, but ran westward as far as Bowness. In that year, the first turret on the Turf Wall was identified at Banks, 52*a*, embodied in the Stone Wall; and in 1934 followed the identification of turrets 49*b* TW and 50*a* TW in the Turf Wall itself. These turrets are of stone, twenty feet square, with plinths at back and front and without ladder-platforms. They thus not only match those of the Broad Wall in pre-dating the Narrow Wall, but their different design indicates that they were the counterpart of the Broad Wall turret, while 49*b* TW and 50*a* TW were dismantled when the Narrow Wall was built. In 1934 was also examined the sole unencumbered Turf-Wall milecastle, 50 TW, which closely resembles a Stone-Wall milecastle in plan, but has a turf rampart instead of a stone wall and timber gateways and barrack. Only the north gate had a tower. The occupation was intense but very short. Then a demolition party, burying its rubbish (including a wooden writing-tablet, bracken and heather bedding, an old shoe, etc.) in pits, let fall into one of them a chip from the wooden dedication tablet of the milecastle, bearing part of the names of Hadrian and Platorius Nepos, and now at Tullie House Museum, Carlisle. The whole text was shown by the late Professor R. G. Collingwood to match that of the stone tablets from Cawfields and Hotbank. This evidence shows that the Turf Wall was Hadrianic but was quickly replaced by the Narrow Wall, itself proved Hadrianic in 1911.

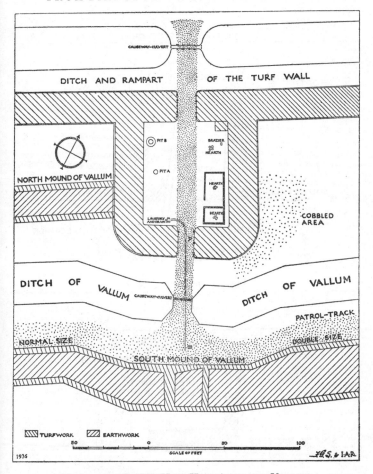

MILECASTLE 50 TW (HIGH HOUSE) AND THE VALLUM.

The Vallum runs close behind the Turf Wall throughout
this sector. At milecastles 49 and 50 TW, it is so close that
the north mound is omitted and replaced by a south mound
of double size, thus proving that the Vallum is later than the
Turf Wall hereabouts. At milecastle 50 TW the north mound

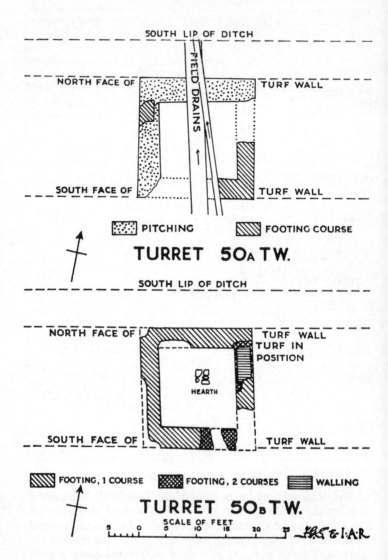

SOUTH LIP OF DITCH

FIELD DRAINS

NORTH FACE OF   TURF WALL

SOUTH FACE OF   TURF WALL

▓ PITCHING   ▨ FOOTING COURSE

TURRET 50ᴀ T.W.

SOUTH LIP OF DITCH

NORTH FACE OF   TURF WALL
TURF IN POSITION

HEARTH

SOUTH FACE OF   TURF WALL

▨ FOOTING, 1 COURSE   ▩ FOOTING, 2 COURSES   ▤ WALLING

TURRET 50ʙ T.W.

SCALE OF FEET
5   0   5   10   15   20   25   F.G.S. & I.A.R.

begins again and the ditch and south mound make a south-ward diversion. The ditch was originally interrupted by a causeway revetted in stone, as at the forts, leading, however, not to a gap in the south mound but to a patrol-track on the south berm of the Vallum. Later, after the demolition of the milecastle, the causeway was replaced by a wide crossing and a roadway through the south mound; but this roadway was finally blocked by embankments, restoring the ditch. The discovery of the patrol-track and its intimate connexion with the milecastle defines the place of the Vallum as the rearward patrolled boundary of the military zone associated with the Wall. The obliteration of the causeway is no doubt connected with the dismantling of milecastle doors in A.D. 140, while the embankments go with the rehabilitation of the barrier.

West of milecastle 50 TW, in the neighbourhood of High House, the Vallum is in excellent preservation. The usual gaps are visible in the north mound, and traces of causeways are seen in the ditch; but in the south mound, as at Shield-on-the-Wall and Wallend Common (pp. 107, 155) only notches indicate where gaps were to come, as also on the Turf Wall, though there are substantial causeways in its ditch.

Just beyond the site of turret 50b and opposite Appletree barn, a lane goes off to south; 150 yards down this lane a section has been cut through the Turf Wall, showing its laminated structure, in blocks of whitish bleached roots and humus alternating with streaks of dark carbonised grass. Individual turves can often by recognised.

At milecastle 51 (Wall Bowers) the Stone Wall once more rejoins the line of the Turf Wall and crosses its filled-up ditch. The milecastle is girt by a ditch as at milecastles 23, 25 and 29, though it has never been completely dug. Like milecastles 47 and 48, Wall Bowers had two stone barracks. Its south gate, of type III, had been rebuilt in the fourth century with large monolithic jambs and a massive threshold set in a deep trench. The Vallum runs some distance behind the mile-castle and had been originally furnished with a stone-revetted causeway, which had later been replaced by a wider crossing and road across the south mound, all as at milecastle 50 TW.

South of Wall Bowers, across the Irthing, is Nether Denton church, on a hillock occupied by a Roman fort of the early Stanegate series. Its turf rampart, found in 1933 to be 30 feet thick, lies below the south wall of the church-yard, and its extra-mural bath-house was found when the present vicarage was built in 1868. Coins and pottery, found on the site in 1868, 1911 and 1933, show that it was occupied intensively from Agricolan times until the first years of the Wall, serving as one of the first-phase Wall-forts.

It was at first supposed that the Turf Wall ended at Wall Bowers; but it is now proved to extend to Bowness-on-Solway, by the following facts. While the Stone-Wall turrets are an integral part of its structure, with wing-walls for bonding, the Turf-Wall turrets, as was proved by excavating those corresponding to 50a and 50b, were square stone towers with a plinth at back and front and the Turf Wall abutting on either side. In 1927, turrets 51a, 51b and 52a were found to be stone towers of Turf-Wall type, incorporated in the Stone Wall, which butted against their east and west walls with a straight joint some three feet behind their north face. Further excavation revealed actual traces of the dismantled Turf Wall in contact with them. Similar proof was then obtained at turret 79b, just east of Bowness.

West of Wall Bowers, at a lodge south of the road, a path leads to Coombe Crag, a freestone quarry extensively worked by the Romans. The soldiers have left inscriptions on the face of the rock, including the names SECVRVS, IVSTVS, and MATERNVS. An inscription at the foot of the cliff, reading FAVST ET RVF COS and purporting to mention Faustinus and Rufus, the consuls of A.D. 210, is a forgery, perpetrated to suggest that the Wall was built in the reign of Severus. It can be seen how relatively fresh is the punching of the letters, and how different in style from genuine inscriptions. South of Coombe Crag, at Lanerton, further quarry inscriptions, seen by Hodgson, have now vanished.

Immediately west of Coombe Crag Wood the Vallum is in its original condition for about 800 yards: there is no gap in the mounds, no causeway in the ditch, and no marginal mound. Only here and at Limestone Corner (p. 98) can the Vallum be seen entirely free from alteration.

The south walls of turrets 51*a* and 51*b* are visible in the north verge of the modern road, and their close proximity to the Wall-ditch, typical of the Turf-Wall structures, will be appreciated. Turret 51*b*, examined in 1958, was dismantled under Severus and casually re-occupied late in the fourth century. Next comes the site of milecastle 52 (Bankshead). Here were discovered in 1808 two altars to the local deity Cocidius, now in Lanercost Priory, and in 1862 a broken slab on which had been roughly scabbled the name of Antoninus Pius. One altar to Cocidius, here figured, was dedicated by soldiers of the Twentieth Legion in the years 262-6, Aper and Rufus being consuls of the separatist Gallic Empire, to which Britain adhered. Excavation in 1934 proved milecastle 52 to have been exceptionally large, 76 feet 9 inches from north to south by 90 feet 3 inches from east to west internally. Its north gate, of type III, having received new pivot-stones in the second century, was reduced to a foot-way in the third and blocked late in the fourth. The south gate, as at mile-

ALTAR TO COCIDIUS FROM MILECASTLE 52 (BANKSHEAD), AT LANERCOST PRIORY.

castle 51, was completely remodelled in the fourth century by the insertion of large stone jambs and threshold; and some of the iron strapping from the doors was found.

The extra large size of milecastle 52 is explained by the remains next seen on Pike Hill, the summit of the ridge here occupied by the Wall, with a view embracing North Cumberland and beyond. On it stood a Roman signal-tower, twenty feet square, which was not part of the turret-system of the Wall, for turret 52*a* lies only some 200 yards to west. The tower is also orientated forty-five degrees away from the

Wall-line, while the Turf Wall, its ditch and the later Stone Wall all make a zig-zag to fit it. The explanation of this curious planning lies in the relation of the tower to other points. As placed, its two eastward sides face Gillalees watch-tower, Nether Denton fort, and Walltown turret (45*a*), the other known turret of this type (p. 151); its two westward sides face Boothby fort on the Stanegate and the outpost fort

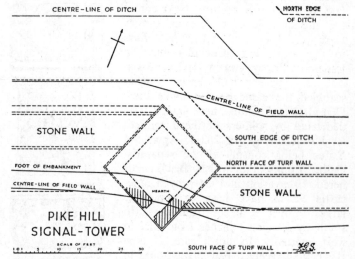

at Netherby. Its exceptionally deep foundations seem to denote extra height, and its purpose may well have been fast long-distance signalling, cutting out the normal patrol-signals of the Wall.

Turret 52*a*, less than 100 yards west of Pike Hill, is now displayed, under Ministry guardianship. It is a fine example of a Turf-Wall turret, with the characteristic plinth visible at front and back and the Stone Wall abutting upon it. It stands 14 courses high and a fallen piece of the superstructure lies just west of it. The demolished Turf Wall was found to abut against its east wall. The turret was intensively occupied until A.D. 296, after which it appears to have been used as a pent-house, with the Wall carried across it to full width.

Before coming to the brook called Banks Burn, a piece of the core of the Wall is seen. Here is the measured position of milecastle 53 (Banks Burn); but it was in fact placed on better ground, at Banks Burn farm house west of the stream. Its gates were of type III and its internal dimensions 76½ feet from north to south and 72 feet from east to west. In 1932 a fragment of the levelled Turf Wall was found inside it. Ascending Hare Hill the Wall stands nine feet ten inches high. The core is original, the facing a preservative measure of the nineteenth century. A centurial stone, recording the century of the *primus pilus* or senior centurion of the first cohort, found at Moneyholes, two fields further west, is placed in the north face. This is the highest piece of the Wall visible anywhere, and has been so for two centuries. " I viewed this relic with admiration. I saw no part higher ", wrote Hutton.

The road leading downhill to Lanercost Priory passes along the east edge of a ravine, in which a rock-face bears a forged inscription reading " I. Brutus, decurion in the *Ala Petriana* ". It was once wrongly believed that Lanercost was a Roman site garrisoned by this unit; and the forgery was an attempt to bolster up the notion.

Lanercost Priory, an Augustinian house of 1169, is of great beauty and charmingly situated near the Irthing. Its nave is still a church, the rest is in the custody of the Ministry of Public Building and Works. Built almost entirely of red and grey stones from the Wall, it contains an altar to Jupiter, from Birdoswald, in the headway of the clear story passage at the south-east angle of the choir. One to Silvanus from Birdoswald and two to Cocidius from milecastle 52 are in the undercroft south of the church. A fine eighteenth-century bridge leads over the river to Naworth Castle, the seat of the Earls of Carlisle; upstream are remains of an older bridge, once thought Roman, but in fact medieval.

The Quarry Beck, which joins the Irthing at Lanercost Bridge, is crossed by the Stanegate in deep cuttings to east and west of the Naworth Estate sawmill. This is a good example of the embanking and cutting by which the Roman engineers negotiated deep ravines. East of Naworth Castle, Pottscleugh is crossed by a very elaborate embankment and cuttings, in all about 350 yards long. West of Quarry Beck the general course of the road was by Boothby, Great Easby and Brecon Hill to Irthington. At Boothby Castle Hill excavation in 1933 revealed a small Stanegate fort, comparable with Throp and associated with early Hadrianic pottery.

About two hundred yards west of Hare Hill a break in the Wall occurs, in which a turret or small quadrangular building has been situated. This building projects beyond the Wall, northwards, rather less than three feet. It is constructed of smaller stones than the Wall; the workmanship of it is excellent. It measures fourteen feet six inches (inside measurement) from east to west. When first noticed it was full of black ashes; the discoverers took it to be a smithy. Altogether it is a peculiar building; though it has some of the features of a turret, it seems to have been built independently of the Wall.

The previous paragraph, left much as Bruce wrote it, shows how accurately he described a building which is in fact Turf-Wall turret 53a, with the Narrow Wall brought up to its east and west sides and later covered by the medieval boundary-wall of Lanercost Priory lands. The spot has been wrongly named Moneyholes, which really lies 150 yards farther west, where treasure has been sought in vain. Through the Priory Woods, to south, the Vallum runs straight westward, in good condition.

At Craggle Hill the Wall ditch is very bold. Turret 53b, of Turf-Wall type and built in red sandstone instead of yellow freestone, has been found here. At Hayton Gate a track, once a drove road, crosses the Wall, approximately on the line of the Red Rock Fault, the great geological cleavage between the limestone and the red sandstone. West of this point no limestone is obtainable anywhere near the Wall and this fact induced the change from Stone Wall to Turf Wall in the original design.

Just west of Randylands comes milecastle 54, excavated in 1934, measuring internally 77½ feet from north to south and 64¼ feet from east to west. Its gates, of type III, were reduced

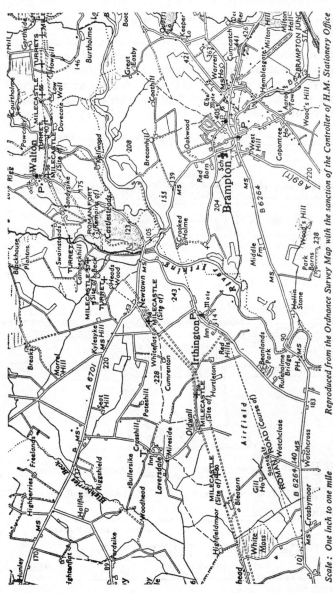

Reproduced from the Ordnance Survey Map with the sanction of the Controller of H.M. Stationery Office

9. GARTHSIDE—HOWGILL—CASTLESTEADS

Scale: One inch to one mile

to posterns under Severus after renewal of pivot-blocks in the second century. A west barrack comprised two rooms, one fitted with stone benches, hearth and millstone, the other empty. Beneath the stone milecastle, but on an axis somewhat to east, lay the Turf-Wall milecastle, built in beaten clay owing to deficiency of good turf. This clay construction

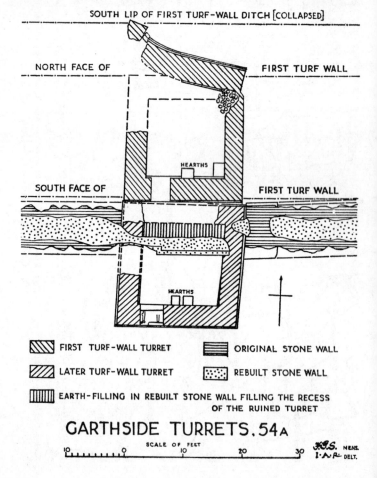

SOUTH LIP OF FIRST TURF-WALL DITCH [COLLAPSED]

NORTH FACE OF   FIRST TURF WALL

HEARTHS

SOUTH FACE OF   FIRST TURF WALL

HEARTHS

⬚ FIRST TURF-WALL TURRET   ▤ ORIGINAL STONE WALL

▨ LATER TURF-WALL TURRET   ⸱⸱⸱ REBUILT STONE WALL

▥ EARTH-FILLING IN REBUILT STONE WALL FILLING THE RECESS
   OF THE RUINED TURRET

GARTHSIDE TURRETS, 54A

SCALE OF FEET
10   0   10   20   30

ℋℐℒ. MENS.
I·A·ℛ DELT.

continues in the so-called Turf Wall itself for about half a mile to the west. After the crossing of Burtholme Beck a piece of the Wall stands nearly seven feet high; its facing-stones are gone, but the hard white mortar possesses its original tenacity. This quality of mortar is typical of the Severan reconstruction of the Wall. Here too a change in the structure of the Wall may be noted. From this point to Bowness the flag-footing is 9 feet 3 inches wide at least and carries a Wall 8½ feet thick, as compared with the Narrow Wall which is 7½ feet thick. This Intermediate Wall represents the replacement of the Turf Wall over the greater part of its length by an operation distinct from and later than the building of the Narrow Wall.

At turret 54a a remarkable building-sequence underlines the later building of the Intermediate Wall. As the Wall-ditch approaches the turret from Burtholme Beck, it will be observed swinging northwards and taking the bottom of the northward slope. This arrangement is secondary. The older ditch, still outlined in certain conditions of growth, followed the Wall to the turret, excavated in 1933, when the reason for the change became plain. There had been two turrets. The one, a Clay-Wall turret, had collapsed into the ditch, owing to unstable subsoil, after a measure of use. A new Wall, this time of turf, was then built further north, with the secondary ditch, while a second turret was built behind the old one as an isolated tower. Later came the Stone Wall, incorporating the second turret. Finally, when this Wall was destroyed in A.D. 197, the Severan Stone Wall was built, without any turret, across the ruins of the second building. This complicated story provides ample proof that the Turf Wall here lasted for some time: its replacement in stone is of the second-century, but not immediate.

The Wall runs north of Howgill, by Low Wall and Dove-cote, on its way to the King Water. In the wall of an out-house at Howgill there is a rough inscription recording work by the Catuvellauni of Hertfordshire. Turret 54b, at 535 yards west of turret 54a, is a Turf-Wall turret, and some turf-work was found at its east side in 1933. Nearly due north of Low

Wall are slight indications of milecastle 55, partly excavated in 1900, when it yielded later fourth century pottery. Turret 55*a*, found in 1933 528 yards west of milecastle 55, is again a Turf-Wall turret. The Wall now becomes difficult to follow through the arable fields, but the road by Dovecote comes back to it before crossing the King Water. Here, the ditch of the Wall is seen climbing the hill to Walton, and the berm widens, doubtless because sandy subsoil threatened trouble, as at Garthside. Through Walton its general course lies below the Black Bull Inn, and milecastle 56 (Walton) is wholly obliterated. On the village green Horsley saw traces of a temporary camp. The Wall was next located at Sandysike in 1933, on deep masonry foundations near the stream; and

BUILDING-STONE OF A BRITISH TRIBAL *corvée*, AT HOWGILL.

Turf-Wall turret 56*b* was also found, between the farm and the Cambeck, with traces of the demolished Turf Wall. The Intermediate Stone Wall is here 9 feet 6 inches wide across its flag footing, and, with the wide berm already noted, crosses the Cambeck at the weir.

The Vallum, following a straight line from Banks Burn, was traced by excavation in 1900 from Low Wall to a point about 300 yards south-east of the Black Bull Inn at Walton, on the north edge of Crowhall wood, when it turned sharply south. By another southward turn, half a mile farther on, it deviated round the south side of the fort at Castlesteads, and turned west again to converge with the Wall beyond the Cambeck.

The Roman quarries on the river Gelt, with their inscriptions, lie about four miles to the south of this point. The most famous of the inscriptions, the "Written Rock", has already been noted (p. 35). Half a mile higher up the river, on the opposite side, is the quarry face of Pigeon Crag, with the names of men from the Sixth Legion. In Cumberland, the quarries which supplied the Wall are generally further away than in Northumberland, though at Cambeck and at Bleatarn the soft red sandstone available on the spot was used.

FORT XIII   CASTLESTEADS (UXELLODUNUM)

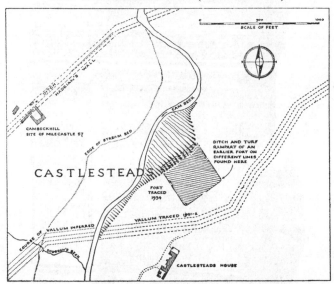

SITE OF CASTLESTEADS FORT, 1934.

Castlesteads fort, almost seven miles from Birdoswald, lies on a high bluff, commanding the Cambeck valley and the important break in the mosses to north-west which carries the modern road from Brampton to Longtown. It thus guards an important line of approach to the Wall and also watches the east bank of the Cambeck against raiders from the Bewcastle area. The site, however, was levelled in 1791, when the gardens of Castlesteads House were laid over it. The Rudge Cup and Amiens skillet, which name the important Wall-forts from the west to Birdoswald, here supply the name

Uxel(l)odu(nu)m, which, meaning "lofty fort", would suit the site well. At Uxellodunum in the early fourth century the *Notitia* places the First cohort of Spaniards; while Castlesteads inscriptions suggest that its garrison may have been, in the second century, the First cohort of Batavians and the

ALTAR OF THE SECOND COHORT OF TUNGRIANS, AT CASTLESTEADS.

Fourth cohort of Gauls, and in the third, the Second cohort of Tungrians, presumably not at full strength, since the full unit, one thousand strong, would not fit into so small a fort. Excavations in 1934 revealed the east, west and south wall, defended by a single ditch, and the east and west double gates. The north-west front had been eroded by the Cambeck.

From east to west the fort measures 394 feet over its rampart and is thought to have been originally about 400 feet square, covering some 3¾ acres. The stone fort was not the earliest on the site. Remains of a turf rampart and earlier ditch-system, found at the south-east angle, no doubt belong to the first fort on the line of the Wall, replacing the Stanegate fort at Old Church.

Interesting altars are preserved in the summer-house, together with a few stones from other sites. The finest is the altar to Jupiter, translated as "To Jupiter, Best and Greatest, the Second milliary cohort of Tungrians, with mounted detachment, Latin citizens, commanded by Albius Severus, prefect of the Tungrians; Victorius Severus, senior centurion, in charge of the task". The altar inscribed DISCIPVLINAE AVGVSTI is also interesting and matched by others at Greatchesters, Corbridge, Birrens and Bewcastle. Its inscription originally ended AVGGG, with reference to the three emperors, Severus, Caracalla and Geta, reigning from A.D. 209-211; after the murder of Geta in A.D. 212, Severus already being dead, it was altered as we see it. The site also

ALTAR TO DISCIPLINE OF A.D. 209-211, AT CASTLESTEADS.

yielded three altars to Mithras, while not far from it an altar dedicated to the north-British god Maponus by four German irregulars, was found about 1690.

Castlesteads is the only fort which stands in a southward deviation of the Vallum but is not in contact with the Wall. The engineers chose the fort-site for outlook and impregnability, while the Wall had already been taken by easier gradients to a sound crossing of the Cambeck, where rock replaces alluvial flats. Anyone seeing the Cambeck in spate will agree that the choice was right.

FROM CASTLESTEADS TO STANWIX

The early site on the Stanegate corresponding to Castlesteads lay at St. Martin's Old Church, Brampton, on a steep bluff east of the Irthing. This fort, almost 400 feet square, was partly excavated in 1935. It had a single ditch, a turf

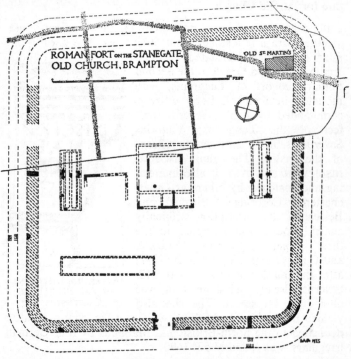

ROMAN FORT on the STANEGATE, OLD CHURCH, BRAMPTON

OLD St MARTIN'S

rampart and stone buildings, including *principia,* granaries and barracks. It is connected with the Stanegate, which runs in the flats to north, by a road descending in a deep cutting to an embankment across the old river-bed at Crooked Holme. To south the ridge towards Irthing Valley School carries many native agricultural settlements, as air-photography shows. In the school playing-field six tile-kilns and two pottery kilns of Trajanic date were excavated in 1963-4.

On returning to the Wall at the Cambeck, the ditch is seen cutting deep into the red sandstone of the west bank. Cambeckhill farm house covers the site of milecastle 57. The ditch is also well seen to west of the farm buildings at Beck, which are partly constructed of Roman stones. Turret 57*a*, located in 1933, is a Turf-Wall turret. The Intermediate Stone Wall was here 9 feet 6 inches wide across its flag footing.

Headswood occupies a commanding situation above the valley. The ditch is seen approaching from the north-east and on its north side is part of a Norman motte and bailey. The Wall itself, however, here lacks command to northward. About two hundred yards west of Newtown of Irthington, the site of milecastle 58 is evident. At White Flat, the rubble foundation of the Wall is discernible and the ditch very deep. The Wall now follows a field-path south-west of White Flat, where a long strip of the Wall, in fair state, forms a field boundary planted with oak trees.

CENTURIAL STONE FROM OLD WALL, AT CUMRENTON.

Opposite Hurtleton farm house the Wall and Vallum are only thirty-five yards apart; the ditch of each is evident, and for a short distance the Vallum ditch is embanked through a marsh, as at White Moss, described below. At Chapel Flat the field-path ends and both works bend northward. The site of milecastle 59 (Old Wall) is a quarter of a mile beyond the turn. In the farm buildings here are many Roman stones; but a centurial stone of " The Second Legion Augusta, century of Julius Tertullianus " is now at Cumrenton farm house. The Wall is obliterated, but its ditch appears between the road and the buildings.

From this point westward the works may be traced for some distance and an ancient drove-road occupies the site of the Wall. At the end of this lane, however, tall hedges and

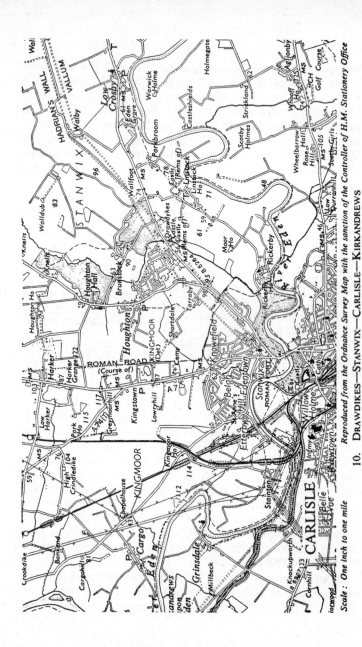

10. DRAWDIKES—STANWIX—CARLISLE—KIRKANDREWS

Scale : One inch to one mile

cultivated fields make the work difficult to follow. A spot called High Strand, the traditional site of milecastle 60, yielded in 1851 an altar to Cocidius, erected by the Sixth Legion and now at Castlesteads.

A mile to south, at Watchcross, is a Roman temporary camp, long known but long lost, one and a half acres in area. It lies south of the Stanegate, which crossed the river near Irthington and ran through a large cutting visible at Buckjumping (west of Redhills) in a straight line towards High

TOMBSTONE FROM STANWIX, AT DRAWDIKES.

Crosby. There, to south of the Carlisle road, it swerves south of the highest point in the hamlet in yet another deep cutting, where the pottery found suggests a small fort, intermediate between Old Church and Stanwix. Further south, on the west of the Eden, Roman quarry inscriptions are visible just south of the Cells, Wetheral, a beauty-spot conserved by the National Trust.

At Bleatarn, the Wall runs a little to north of the farm house, the Vallum immediately south of it. Between Wall and Vallum, and west of the farm house, a large mound carried a belvedere erected by "Nabob" William Richardson about the end of the eighteenth century. Excavations in 1895 proved Bleatarn to be the site of a quarry used for building the Wall.

On White Moss, a little further west, the Vallum ditch, as at Hurtleton, is defined by two mounds; in the marsh its steep sides would have been in danger of collapsing, and were therefore constructed by building up a mound at either side, above ground, instead of digging into the marsh. A section of the Military Way made here in 1894, revealed a gravelled road 22 feet wide, with kerbs, axial rib and lateral ditches.

The measured position of milecastle 61 (Wallhead) is a little east of Wallhead farm, west of which the ditch of the Wall is again in good condition. About six hundred yards east of Walby, where the road turns sharply to north, is the site of milecastle 62 (Walby East); and at Walby itself pools mark the Wall ditch. Here the Wall bends south and, three-quarters of a mile farther on, 500 yards west of the presumed site of milecastle 63 (Walby West), the Vallum almost shaves the Wall without changing course. Nothing is known as yet in this sector of turrets.

In Brunstock Park the lines of the Wall and Vallum ditches are visible as gentle depressions. Excavation here in 1894 confirmed the flat-bottomed section of the Vallum ditch, as found in 1893 at Heddon-on-the-Wall, and also revealed the Military Way, as at White Moss.

The measured position of milecastle 64 (Drawdikes) is opposite Drawdikes Castle. But the site of the Wall west of Drawdikes Beck is occupied by the military, in Hadrian's Camp. Immediately west of Drawdikes Castle the lines of the Vallum are well seen in Drawdikes plantation. The three large busts crowning Drawdikes Castle, connected in local story with the devil and two nineteenth-century local celebrities, are not Roman. A tombstone from Stanwix, built into the south face of the house, is crowned by lions devouring human heads and symbolic of death; its inscription may be translated: " To the spirits of the departed (and) of Marcus Troianius Augustinus; his dearest wife, Aelia Ammillusima, saw to the making (of this tomb)."

The Wall, having run straight for over a mile from near Wallfoot, turns on the crest within Hadrian's Camp, and aims for Stanwix. The line is marked by a broad footpath, running through fields and market gardens. The ditch used to be boldly developed, but is now largely filled up. Two hundred yards beyond Tarraby is the presumed site of milecastle 65 (Tarraby), near which an altar to Cocidius by the Second Legion was used to cover a culvert through the Wall. Fragments of an ornate dedication to Mercury have also been found.

The Vallum runs just south of the main road from Drawdikes to Whiteclosegate. It then crosses the road, turning southward across Knowefield Nurseries, and, entering the garden of Home Acres, must have swung still further south to avoid Stanwix fort. The Military Way runs between Wall and Vallum. Cremation burials were found to south of the Vallum at Whiteclosegae in 1936.

FORT XIV STANWIX (PETRIANA)

Stanwix fort lay on the fine natural platform occupied by Stanwix Church and Stanwix House. The purpose of the site was to guard the Eden bridgehead and to watch the very important western route to and from Scotland. The ground falls away on all sides but the west, and there the Eden, in a wide deep valley, is close at hand. Before the ground was built over the south-east slope near Brampton road and the south slope towards the Eden bridge were covered with buildings, and a road ran from the south gate of the fort, just east of Church Lane, down to the Eden a little east of the present bridge.

The fort is upwards of six miles from Castlesteads. The mound of the south rampart is clear in the churchyard, and the south ditch, with a break at the south gate, was traced in 1933. The south-west angle-tower, south wall and east wall were found in 1940, following the discovery of the west ditches in draining an air-raid shelter. The Wall, forming the north front, was traced in Stanwix School yard in 1932-4. The fort thus covers 580 by 700 feet, far outstripping in size

(9·32 acres) the forts, covering 580 by 400 feet, designed for cavalry 500 strong or infantry 1,000 strong. It may thus be recognised as intended for a cavalry regiment 1,000 strong: and this can only have been the *ala Petriana*, the sole regiment of that size on the Wall. The garrison of the fort and its name. PETRIANA, are thus identified. The exceptional size of the garrison emphasises that this was the most important position on the Wall, the base for aggressive action against the northern tribes and the seat of the senior commandant of the Wall-garrison.

SCULPTURED UPPER PORTION OF A TROOPER'S TOMBSTONE, FROM STANWIX (NETHERHALL).

Little is known of internal buildings, but long barrack-like buildings were found in the school-yard in 1934; while in 1939 a large granary, lying east and west, was found in extending the school-yard and is marked in its pavement. A cavalry-man's tombstone was found in the wall of the old parish church about 1790, though only the dedication of the inscription is left; while in pulling down the old church was found a very fine relief of Victory, now at Newcastle. Another free-standing Victory upon a globe, also at Newcastle, came from outside the fort; while in Tullie House there is a dedication set up in A.D. 167, found to west of the fort in 1931.

In the low ground of Rickerby Park, north of the river, many Roman objects washed down the cliff were discovered in 1934, buried 15 feet deep in river silt. They included brooches, mountings for cavalry-men's uniform and harness, and odds and ends of metal; and had come from a bronze-founder's workshop, in use about the middle of the second century, in the suburbs of the fort.

The Vallum turns south from Knowefield Nurseries through the garden of Home Acres, and has been traced to a point

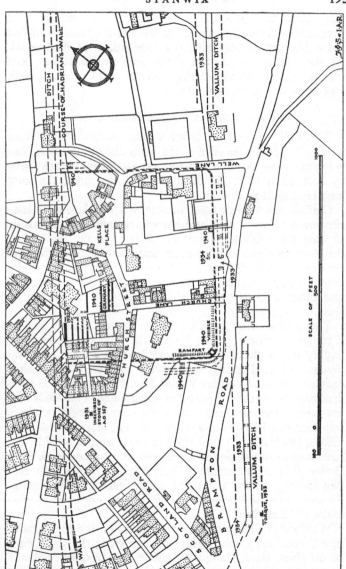

STANWIX FORT, 1940.

just short of the south-east angle of the fort. Here it presumably deviated to avoid the fort and is so close to it that the north mound may have been omitted, as at Birdoswald. At the south-west angle a sharp turn eastwards has been traced, whence the ditch makes for the west end of the Park and turns west towards the Eden.

FROM STANWIX TO BURGH-BY-SANDS

The Wall runs parallel to the Vallum, with the same sharp westward turn, to the edge of the bluffs above the Eden. This is the measured position of milecastle 66 (Stanwix Bank), seen by Pennant in 1772. The ditch is visible descending the scarp near Hyssop Holme Well.

Carlisle, the ancient LUGUVALIUM, is a well-known Roman site and the area of the Cathedral was occupied by a fort from at least Agricola's time until the building of the Wall. Then the place became a town of some size, covering much the same area as its medieval successor. Tullie House Museum contains most valuable collections of Roman objects from the Wall and other Roman sites in Cumberland and should on no account be missed.

The Wall crossed the Eden below Hyssop Holme Well by a bridge. Camden records "within the chanell of the river, mighty stones, the remaines thereof" and when the river was dredged in 1951 many stones were recovered, including a centurial stone of Vesnius Viator. The site lay about 40 yards upstream from the supposed crossing-point. The Wall then ran west-south-westwards across the sewage works, where it was found in 1854, excavated in 1886 and marked with stone pillars, and finally exposed again in 1931, when a considerable stretch of its foundation was removed to the grounds of Tullie House. It is the Intermediate Wall, 8 feet 10 inches wide, on a flag footing. At the south end of the Silloth railway bridge Roman coins have been found, on the presumed site of mile-castle 67 (Stainton).

Wall and Vallum draw together again on the high ground just beyond the engine sheds and run along the south bank of the river. Here, along the bluffs called Davidson's Banks,

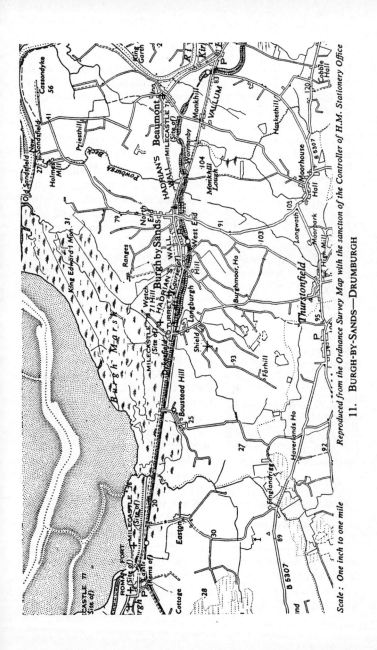

Scale : One inch to one mile

Reproduced from the Ordnance Survey Map with the sanction of the Controller of H.M. Stationery Office

11. BURGH-BY-SANDS—DRUMBURGH

the Wall ran near the river, which probably served as the ditch. The Vallum lies close behind, and at one point four or five gaps, spaced at the usual interval of forty-five yards, can be seen in its north mound.

East of the measured position of milecastle 68 (Boomby Gill) the two works diverge and the Wall keeps to the river-bank as far as Grinsdale, while the Vallum aims straight for Kirkandrews. The Wall ditch is seen crossing the road at the south-west end of Grinsdale; and here the Wall leaves the river and seizes the bluffs that overlook the river flats to north.

LIVNIVSVIC
TORINVS·FL·
CAELIANVS·LEG
AVG·LEG·VI·V·C
P·F·OB·RES·TRANS
VALLVM·PR·O
SPERE·GESTA

ALTAR DEDICATED BY A
LEGIONARY LEGATE, AFTER
OPERATIONS NORTH OF
THE WALL
(TULLIE HOUSE).

About three-quarters of a mile south-west of Grinsdale on rising ground two small Roman camps, each with four gateways of the traverse type, were noted by MacLauchlan and have been seen anew in air-photographs. While at Kirksteads, half a mile west of these camps, was found an altar dedicated by " Lucius Iunius Victorinus Flavius Caelianus, commander of the Victorious, Dutiful and Loyal Sixth Legion, on account of successful operations beyond the Wall " (*ob res trans Vallum prospere gestas*). It is now in Tullie House.

Kirkandrews church-yard, where a twelfth-century church once stood, lies south of the rectory, and is so stony that Bruce thought it might cover a milecastle. But the measured position of milecastle 70 (Braelees) is further north and the stones probably belong to the vanished church.

The Wall now follows the bluffs to Beaumont, dispensing with the ditch until it leaves them at Dolly's Brae. The

Vallum runs straight, by Monkhill and Wormanby, to Burgh-by-Sands, lying south of the modern road to Monkhill and then north of it until the road crosses the railway beyond Wormanby. It is plainly seen in the field between the railway-bridge and Powburgh Beck.

The ditch of the Wall is well developed at Monkhill Beck, before approaching Beaumont, and going up the hill both Wall and ditch are visible. In a wall at Beaumont, to west of the village street, is part of a building-stone of the fifth cohort of the Twentieth Legion, from the Eden. In 1934, an altar was found during demolitions, dedicated to Jupiter and the Genius of the *numerus* of Aurelian Moors, Valerianus' and Gallienus' Own (A.D. 253-58). This stone doubtless came from Burgh-by-Sands, and its bearing upon the name of that fort is considered below.

The church at Beaumont stands upon a mound, which MacLauchlan recognised as a motte, the early medieval castle of the le Brun, or de la Ferté, family. In the west extension of the church-yard the Intermediate Wall was found in 1928: it was about 9 feet wide, its flag footing set upon a foundation of clay and cobbles a foot deep. The stones used for the core came from Stonepot Scar, north of the Solway.

The Wall turns sharply west at Beaumont, running just south of the accommodation road serving the fields to north of the disused railway line. Milecastle 71 was identified in 1960, close to the north-east corner of the large field where the road ends. Thence the Wall ran straight to the site of the fortified manor-house, where it turned westward, as discovered in 1950. It was noted in the modern road in 1877 by A. Mossman, an artist who did much work for Bruce, as making a sharp turn just before reaching the fort, so as to join the fort at right-angles. At Powburgh Beck the Military Way is close behind the Wall and there are traces of a culvert.

FORT XV BURGH-BY-SANDS (ABALLAVA)

The fort of Burgh-by-Sands is five and a half miles from Stanwix and covers between four and a half and five acres. Its function was to guard the southern end of two important

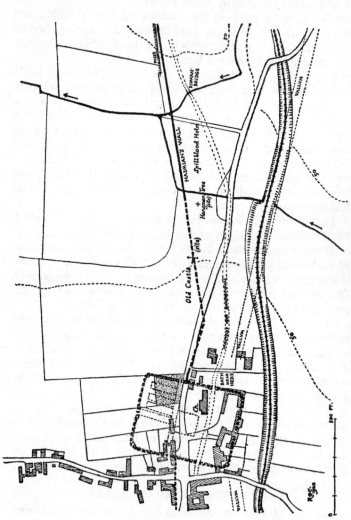

BURGH-BY-SANDS (BROKEN LINES CONJECTURAL).

Solway fords, the Peat Wath and the Sandwath, favourite routes for medieval Border raiders at low water. The site of turret 71*b* seems to lie just at or just within the east gate of the fort, which was found in the south-east corner of the new church-yard, to north of the road running through the village. The bath-house lay to south-east, not far from the vicarage, and was destroyed in making the canal-bed which later carried the railway line, now itself dis-used. The Vallum approached the fort from east and west in such a way as to suggest that it must have made a deviation, though the course has not been traced.

An altar found in 1934 at Beaumont, as noted above, shows that the fort was garrisoned by a *numerus* of Aurelian Moors, irregulars reinforcing the regular cohort in garrison as at Housesteads. The name of the fort is thus ABALLAVA, as recorded by the *Notitia*. A relic of a cohort is a fragmentary second-century altar, dedicated to Hercules and

DEDICATION TO HERCULES
AND THE EMPEROR, AT
BURGH-BY-SANDS.

the deity of the Emperor, which is now built into a stable at Cross Farm. Inscriptions also attest the presence of the *ala I Tungrorum* and the First cohort of Nerva's Own Germani in the second century.

The village church, built almost entirely of Roman stones, is a rare specimen of a fortified Border church. Its west tower is an early fourteenth-century pele-tower, with walls seven feet thick and an original iron grille, or yett, shutting it off from the nave. The east tower, blocking an original east window, is thought to be the late medieval vicarage.

North of the village lies Burgh Marsh, where Edward I was encamped, waiting for a favourable opportunity to cross the Solway, when death seized him on 7 July 1307. A monument erected in 1685 marks the spot where local tradition placed his tent.

FROM BURGH-BY-SANDS TO DRUMBURGH

From Burgh fort the Wall runs slightly south of west for quarter of a mile to the site of milecastle 72 (Fauld Farm), identified in 1960. In the surface of a lane running north from the main road beyond this point, the facing-stones of the Wall may be seen, and the ditch is visible in the fields. Turret 72*a* lies in the measured position at West End and its site yielded pottery. At the lane west of the police station

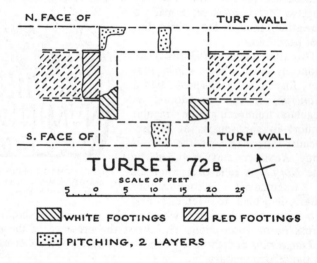

N. FACE OF   TURF WALL

S. FACE OF   TURF WALL

TURRET 72B

SCALE OF FEET

5   0   5   10   15   20   25

▨ WHITE FOOTINGS   ▨ RED FOOTINGS

▨ PITCHING, 2 LAYERS

the Wall turns and runs west-north-westward to Watch Hill, north of Dykesfield. Turret 72*b* was identified in 1948 at the north-east corner of the field north of Rindle House. It was a Turf-Wall turret, projecting four feet north of the Stone Wall. Milecastle 73 (Dykesfield) was then found at the correct measured position, $62\frac{1}{2}$ feet from north to south and $60\frac{2}{3}$ feet from east to west. East of the milecastle traces of the levelled Turf Wall were found in 1934. The Intermediate Wall, 8 feet $8\frac{1}{2}$ inches wide, on a flag footing, then runs straight down to the marsh at Dykesfield. The Vallum at Burgh-by-Sands has been traced from the low ground behind the Greyhound Inn to the west end of the village, and then runs, faintly visible, through the fields to Dykesfield, about fifty yards north of the modern road.

The Wall, when last seen both at Dykesfield and Drumburgh, is making straight for the opposite side of the marsh, over two miles away. It was once thought that it might have skirted the marsh by way of Boustead Hill and Easton; but the location of milecastle 73 makes it clear that the straight course across the Marsh fills the correct distance to milecastle 76. The marsh is probably due to post-Roman transgression.

The Wall, deeply buried in the marsh silt, emerges east of Drumburgh village. Its line crosses the disused railway-siding 150 yards west of the road-bridge over the railway. The site of milecastle 76 (Drumburgh) is marked by a low mound 223 yards east of Drumburgh fort. Here the Wall is running almost due west, and excavation in 1899 traced it up the hill to the fort. It is the Intermediate Wall, nine feet seven inches wide across the footing. The berm and ditch were here found to be some twenty-four feet wide and twenty-six to twenty-nine feet wide respectively.

FORT XVI   DRUMBURGH (CONGAVATA)

Drumburgh fort occupies a bold knoll with excellent outlook over the flatter lands to east and west and the Solway shore to north. Raiders intending to use the Stonewath or the Sandwath fords could be well observed and on occasion interrupted. The site lies four miles west of Burgh-by-Sands and was linked by a Roman road with Kirkbride. Early antiquaries placed a fort on the top of the hill, but did not agree about its size; and were in fact deceived by the deep ditch of the medieval grange occupying the crest. Excavation in 1947 revealed that a Stone fort, whose north-west angle was bonded with the Intermediate Stone Wall, stood inside a fort with clay rampart, measuring over the rampart 270 feet from north to south by 316 feet from east to west. This earthwork fort had been added to the Turf Wall. The size of the Stone fort could not be determined, but pottery attested an occupation after A.D. 369, and its planning was unusual, with a granary in the north-west angle.

There are a few inscriptions and a building-stone reads

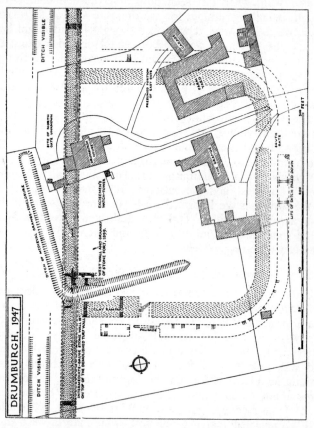

PEDATVRA VINDOMORVCI, marking a length of the Wall built or repaired by Vindomorucus.

Drumburgh Castle, to south of the village street, is a fine old Cumberland manor-house. It was fortified in 1307 by Robert le Brun, but the present house was built by Thomas,

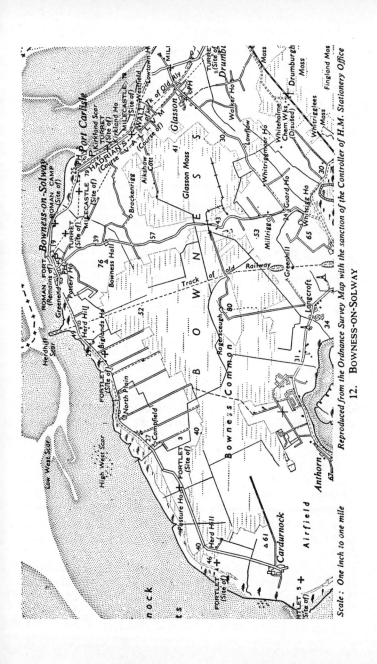

Scale : One inch to one mile

Reproduced from the Ordnance Survey Map with the sanction of the Controller of H.M. Stationery Office

12. BOWNESS-ON-SOLWAY

Lord Dacre under Henry VIII. Leland noted that at " Drumbuygh the Lord Dakers father builded apon old ruines a
prety pyle for defens of the contery . . . The stones of the
Pict Wal were pulled down to build Drumbuygh. For the Wal
ys very nere yt ". The house is in fact almost entirely built
of Roman stones.

FROM DRUMBURGH TO BOWNESS-ON-SOLWAY

As the road leaves Drumburgh the Wall is visible on its
south side, and turret 76a was found in 1948, just east of
Drumburgh school-house. At the school the road turns north-
west, while the Wall goes straight on along a hedge line, and
then itself turns sharply north, to meet the road again before
the railway bridge. Beyond the disused railway, it can be
traced to west of the road. Along the Solway shore, the Wall
runs south of the road to Port Carlisle. The ditch of the Wall
is here omitted. Milecastle 77 (Raven Bank) still awaits
identification.

When the canal was dug, in whose bed later ran the Port
Carlisle railway, now in turn disused, remains of an interglacial forest were discovered near Glasson, and the foundations of the Wall lay on piles three or four feet above the
level of its trees. Some of the piling timber was used for the
jetty at Port Carlisle and the president's chair of the Society
of Antiquaries of Newcastle upon Tyne.

Just west of Glasson, to north of the accommodation-road
to Kirkland, the Vallum reappears and remains bold until it
runs close behind milecastle 78 (Kirkland), identified in 1934.
Sections cut across the Vallum revealed the typical flat-
bottomed ditch and turf-kerbed mounds of normal propor-
tions. East of Glasson its line is taken by a deep drain, almost
as far as the sharp turn in the Wall west of Drumburgh
School.

At Kirkland, Horsley observed turret 78a, rediscovered
in 1948, 100 feet north-west of Kirkland farm-buildings, in
the south hedge of the road. At the beck south-east of Port
Carlisle traces of the Military Way are seen; and over the

door of Hesket House, formerly the "Steam Packet Hotel", is a fragmentary altar, retaining the words MATRIBVS SVIS MILITE[S], dedicated to the *Deae Matres* by a contingent of soldiers. Beyond this, the modern road and the Wall run out again to the sea-shore, the Wall now running a little north-east of the road: and where it hits the shore there is a mound called Fisher's Cross, in which Roman coins have been found; one was seen by MacLauchlan.

The line of the Wall may be traced from this point nearly all the way to Bowness. From Fisher's Cross it runs at first almost due west, swinging south of the road. Excavation in 1930 revealed the Wall-foundation 9 feet 3 inches wide. MacLauchlan noted, at an angle 150 yards west of Fisher's Cross, signs of milecastle 79 (Solway House), excavated in 1949. It is square in plan, measuring internally $57\frac{1}{2}$ feet both ways, with gateways of type II or III. The stone milecastle covered a short-axis Turf-Wall milecastle, measuring in-

ALTAR TO THE
MOTHER-
GODDESSES,
AT PORT
CARLISLE.

ternally $48\frac{1}{4}$ feet by $40\frac{1}{2}$ feet, with staircase-ramp in the south-east corner. The gates of the stone milecastle had been reduced to posterns in the third century. The date of replace-ment of the Turf-Wall milecastle was either just before A.D. 139 or in A.D. 162-163, and there was no early Antonine occupation. Here, on the old sea-shore, no ditch existed and the Turf Wall had been built upon a substantial sea-bank.

On leaving the milecastle, the Wall curves to the north, aiming for Bowness. The Wall, when first seen here by Bruce, was several feet high and gunpowder was used in bringing it down. Horsley reported it hereabouts ten feet high; and excavation 110 feet east of the milecastle in 1949 revealed it as 8 feet 7 inches wide, upon footings 9 feet 2 inches wide, rebuilt in hard white Severan mortar. 245 yards west of the milecastle a massive fragment still stands. Turret 79*b*, excavated in Jeffrey Croft in 1934, proved to be of Turf Wall type: thus showing that the Turf Wall, of which the actual turfwork was last identified at milecastle 79, continued from the Irthing to Bowness.

The Vallum is seen in the fields west of Port Carlisle. After a southward turn, due south of the village, it runs north of Acremire Lane straight for Bowness, but visible remains

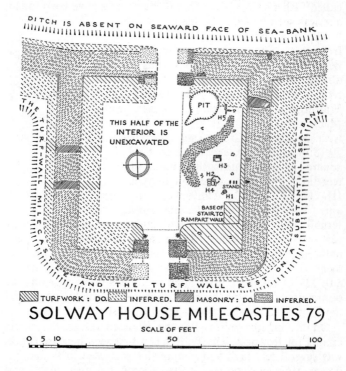

DITCH IS ABSENT ON SEAWARD FACE OF SEA-BANK

THIS HALF OF THE INTERIOR IS UNEXCAVATED

PIT

H5

H3

H2

STAND

H4

H1

BASE OF STAIR TO RAMPART WALK

THE TURF WALL MILECASTLE

AND THE TURF WALL REST ON A SUBSTANTIAL SEA-BANK

▧ TURFWORK: DO.▨ INFERRED. ▧ MASONRY: DO.▨ INFERRED.

SOLWAY HOUSE MILECASTLES 79

SCALE OF FEET

0 5 10   50   100

terminate two fields east of Jeffrey Croft. The ditch, however, has been traced as far as Jeffrey Croft, where it turns sharply southwards as far as Acremire Lane. Nothing further is known of its course, or of how it ended at the coast. Local tradition places the Military Way just behind the Wall as it approaches Bowness.

FORT XVII   BOWNESS-ON-SOLWAY (MAIA)

Bowness, the west terminal fort of the Wall, stands on a sea-cliff a little over fifty feet high, rising steeply from the shore and commanding lower ground in every direction. The cliff forms a rounded promontory, as its name implies, where the estuary ends and the Irish Sea begins. Here, a little east of the fort, was the Stonewath or Bowness Wath, the lowest ford on the Solway, used by John Wesley in 1766. Camden observed, in Holland's words: " I marvailed at first, why they built here so great fortifications, considering that for eight miles, or thereabout, there lieth opposite a very great frith and arme of the sea; but now I understand, that at every ebbe the water is so low, that the borderers and beast-stealers may easily wade over." The present editor has himself seen youths walk across the river from Scotland. Bowness was accordingly chosen as the west end of the Wall.

ALTAR TO JUPITER FOR THE EMPEROR'S WELL-BEING, AT BOWNESS-ON-SOLWAY.

The name of the fort was MAIA, given as *Mais* on the Rudge Cup and Amiens skillet. Its third-century commander was a tribune, implying a milliary cohort of infantry. Its outlines are known. An ancient mound, known as Rampire, or Rampart, Head, lies just outside its east rampart. The west rampart is marked by a re-cut thirteenth-century ditch; and its south-west angle appears faintly. The south rampart was traced by excavation, in 1930, just north of the church-yard. At the same time, by fixing the position of the axial west gate, it was shown that the north rampart lay beyond the present edge of the sea-cliff, and has perished by erosion. The computed size of the fort is 710 by 420 feet, covering over seven acres, making it the second largest on the Wall. The road south to Kirkbride lay some distance west of its present successor, and this fixes the position of the south gate, showing that the fort faced west. The bath-house lay between the two roads opposite the

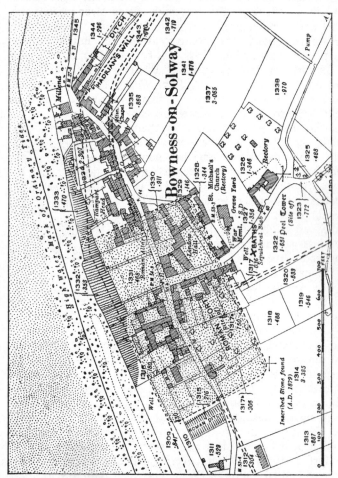

THE SITE OF THE FORT AT BOWNESS-ON-SOLWAY.

church-yard, in a large and prosperous civil settlement, occupied until A.D. 367.

Among inscriptions from the fort, one is seen over a stable door in the main street of the village. It is a small altar to Jupiter, for the welfare of the emperors Gallus and Volusianus, by Sulpicius Secundianus, tribune of an unnamed milliary cohort, of A.D. 251-253. Another still more interesting stone, now at Carlisle, commemorates a trader's vow as he set out upon a venture. The words are in verse, of which the beginning must be supplied, as here in brackets:

> [*Matribus deabus aram Ant*]*onianus dedico:*
> *Sed date ut fetura quaestus suppleat votis fidem:*
> *Aureis sacrabo carmen mox viritim litteris.*

Someone sets up an offering, and adds, " grant that a profitable return may add surety to my vows, I will presently hallow my poem one by one with letters of gold." The final sentiment is inspired by Virgil (*Ecl.* vii, 35-6).

At Wallsend the Wall ran down into the river Tyne as an obstacle to below low-water mark. Of Bowness Reginald Bainbrigg wrote in 1601: " the fundacions of the picts wall may be sene, upon the west skar at a lowe water, covered with sand, a mile and more within the sea, wher the people gett fishe." MacLauchlan records how the stones had been dug out on the beach in the earlier nineteenth century. Many antiquaries noted the submerged interglacial forest.

Four miles south of Bowness a large Roman military site occupies the hill crowned by the church and vicarage of Kirkbride. Recent finds indicate a Trajanic fort, corresponding to those on the Stanegate. Here is to be recognised one of the forts reinforcing the earliest Hadrianic coastal defences, which, like the milecastle and turret system, started without forts on the forward line.

DEFENCES OF THE CUMBERLAND COAST

No account of the Wall is complete without mention of the western shore defences beyond Bowness. Although the Solway cannot be forded farther west, it can be crossed by boat with great ease for several miles westward; and no fortification of the isthmus would be effective which did not provide against this potential danger on the flank.

Accordingly, the Romans continued a chain of posts from Bowness to Moresby. There are four forts, well spaced along the coast, at Beckfoot, Maryport, Burrow Walls and Moresby, the last yielding an inscription of Hadrian not earlier than A.D. 128. The forts, like those on the Wall, were secondary, interjected among a regularly-spaced series of mile-fortlets and towers, whose spacing everywhere corresponds to turret-intervals. Tower 2*b* has been seen from the air, and towers 3*a* and 3*b* were recognised in 1880, stones from 3*a* being built into the gable-end of an outhouse at Pasture House. Beyond the estuary of the Waver and Wampool further towers have now been identified at positions 12*b*, 13*a*, 13*b*, 14*a*, 15*a*, 16*a*, 16*b*, 21*b*, 22*b* and 25*b*, the last at Risehow, south of Maryport.

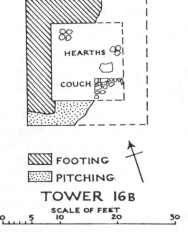

FOOTING

PITCHING.

TOWER 16B

SCALE OF FEET

0   5   10   20   30

Mile-fortlets have been identified as follows: 1 (Bigland), 3 (Pasture House), 4 (Herd Hill), 5 (Cardurnock), 9 (Skinburness), 15 (Beckfoot), 21 (Swarthy Hill) and 22 (Brownrigg). Pasture House and Herd Hill fortlets had turf ramparts. Cardurnock, excavated in 1944, measured 178 by 142 feet over its 28-foot turf rampart, surrounded by a ditch 17 feet wide and entered by a single narrow gateway. Inside were two timber barracks of Hadrianic date. In the second century, during the re-occupation of Scotland, the fortlet was reduced to 144 by 120 feet by building a new rampart on two sides, leaving room for one barrack only. It was apparently not occupied during the third century, but the seaward rampart was refaced with new turf-work in the fourth, occupation continuing after 367. The sites of fortlets 16, 21, 23, 26, 29, 35

CARDURNOCK, MILE FORTLET 5

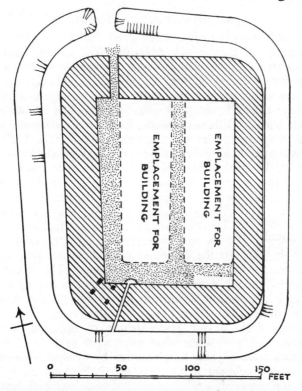

EMPLACEMENT FOR BUILDING

EMPLACEMENT FOR BUILDING

0   50   100   150 FEET

and 36 have also been located by fieldwork. If the arrangement were tidy, mile-fortlet 40 would stand on St. Bee's Head and mark the terminus of the system.

It is thus clear that the Romans treated the Cumberland coast as they treated the banks of the great frontier rivers, such as the Danube, providing it, not with a continuous barrier, which was unnecessary, but with regularly-spaced look-out posts and patrols, to watch for any attempt at a landing. As on the Wall, the forts held fighting garrisons to repel raiders and have been added to the system of mile-fortlets and towers when the original scheme was revised.

THE OUTPOST FORTS TO NORTH

From Newcastle to the North Tyne, and thence almost to milecastle 54, the outlook from the Wall to the north is everywhere so good, that it would be possible to detect an approaching enemy in time to prepare an interception. In Cumberland conditions are mostly different. North of Birdos-wald an enemy could work round the shoulder of the fells which end in Gillalees Beacon; between Castlesteads and Stanwix he could lurk in the mosses and woodland of the Cumberland plain; while beyond the Solway he could concen-trate on the north shore, behind the screen of low hills. The Wall is thus a blind organism, and, to obviate the disadvant-age, outpost forts were provided at Bewcastle, beyond Gillalees, at Netherby, beyond Stanwix, and at Birrens, beyond Solway. The two first are known as Hadrianic from inscriptions, the third from pottery associated with its defences, found in 1937. At the Hadrianic stage, however, little more is known of the sites than their existence. The tower on Gillalees, already described (p. 169) shows how they could be used in preparing a surprise interception of the enemy.

All these sites, except perhaps Bewcastle, served as Antonine forts in the re-occupation of Scotland. Under Severus, they took their place once more as outpost forts. But they were by now supplemented by forts at Risingham and High Rochester in the east, and it becomes clear that from now onwards a wide garrisoned zone was held beyond the Wall. The outpost forts were strongly garrisoned with part-mounted milliary cohorts (Netherby has an inscription commemorating a cavalry drill-hall) and also served as head-quarters for a wide system of patrols. Interception of enemy forces beyond the Wall is thus made possible upon an entirely new and larger scale, while the Wall remains a barrier against infiltration. This fits in with the contemporary reduction of milecastle gateways to posterns, since interception on a large scale was now based not on the Wall but upon the forts in the occupied zone beyond it. This remarkable system lasted until well on into the fourth century. It was then gradually given up. Bewcastle was reconstructed after 297, and both it and Risingham were again reconstructed before 367, probably in 343. High Rochester, however, received no second fourth-century reconstruction, while the closing date for Birrens and Netherby is not yet determined. But the cession of these outpost forts corresponds to political changes. The tribes beyond them had now entered into peaceful relationship with Rome and could be trusted not to become aggressors; a fact which prepares us for the ultimate abandonment of the Wall itself at the close of the century.

[THE END]

APPENDIX

BIBLIOGRAPHY

The purpose of this bibliography is to give references to original first-hand accounts of excavations or discoveries on the line of the Wall. It is not intended to be an exhaustive list of all literature upon each site.

ABBREVIATIONS

AA[1 4] = *Archaeologia Aeliana*, series 1-4.

B[1 3] = Bruce, *Roman Wall*, ed. 1 (1851), 2 (1853), 3 (1867).

CW[1 2] = *Transactions of the Cumberland and Westmorland Archæological and Antiquarian Society*, series 1-2.

DUJ = *Durham University Journal*.

H = Horsley, *Britannia Romana* (1732).

JRS = *Journal of Roman Studies*.

M = MacLauchlan, *Memoir written during a Survey of the Roman Wall* (1858).

NCH = *Northumberland County History*.

OS = Ordnance Survey *Map of Hadrian's Wall* on a scale of 2 inches to the mile, 1964.

PSAN[1 4] = *Proceedings* of the Society of Antiquaries of Newcastle upon Tyne, series 1-4.

RHW = E. Birley, *Research on Hadrian's Wall* (1961).

RIB = R. G. Collingwood & R. P. Wright, *The Roman inscriptions of Britain* (Oxford, 1965).

ANCIENT GEOGRAPHICAL SOURCES

The Antonine Itinerary: O. Cuntz, *Itinerarium Antonini; Itineraria Romana*, vol. I. (Leipzig, 1929).

The Notitia Dignitatum: O. Seeck, *Notitia Dignitatum* (Berlin, 1876).

The Ravenna List: *Archaeologia*, xciii 1.

The Rudge Cup: AA[4] xii 310.

The Amiens skillet: JRS xli 22.

Fort I.   Wallsend

NCH xiii 485-493.
Fort at South Shields, AA⁴ xi 83.
Hadrianic war-memorial, AA⁴ xxi 93.

From Wallsend to Newcastle

NCH xiii 493-501.
Milecastle-sites, AA⁴ xxxviii 40.

Fort II.   Newcastle upon Tyne

NCH xiii, 501-514, RHW, 161.

From Newcastle to Benwell

NCH xiii 515-521.
Wall at Mining Inst., JRS xliii 110.
Ditch in Westgate, AA⁴ xi 227-233.

Fort III.   Benwell

General account: NCH xiii 521-527.
Excavation reports: (1926-1927) AA⁴ iv 135-192, v 46-74;
        (1937) AA⁴ xix 1-43 (1959), AA⁴ xxxviii 233.
Inscription of Hadrian: AA⁴ xix 19, RIB 1340.
Baths: Brand, *History of Newcastle,* i 607.
Praetentura: AA² iii 47.
Vallum causeway: AA⁴ xi 177.
Temple of Antenociticus: AA⁴ xix 37.
Posting-house: AA⁴ v 52.

From Benwell to Rudchester

Throckley hoard: AA⁴ viii 12.
Wall-ditch AA⁴ xxxvi 55.
NCH xiii 527-540, goes to turret 12*b*.
Vallum inscriptions: West Denton, AA⁴ xiv 227, JRS xliv 105;
        ditch, West Denton, AA⁴ xl 135; Mound revetted,
        Heddon, AA⁴ xl 142.
Milecastle 13: M 16, B³ 125, AA⁴ viii 319-322.
    Turret 13*a*: AA⁴ viii 322.

Fort IV.   Rudchester

General accounts: H 139, M 15, B³ 125.
Excavation report (1924): AA⁴ i 93-120.

Course of Vallum: CW¹ xv 178.
Wall-ditch below fort: CW² ii 391.
Gold and silver coin hoard: AA³ viii 219.
Mithraeum: AA⁴ xxxii 176.

FROM RUDCHESTER TO HALTONCHESTERS

Wall with moulded plinth: AA⁴ i 103.
Milecastle 14: M 16, B³ 129.
    High Seat: M 90.
    Turret 14*a*: Horsley, map.
Milecastle 15: H's map, B³ 130.
Milecastle 16: H 141, M 18, B³ 130.
Welton milestone: AA⁴ xvi 255, RIB 2298.
Milecastle 17: H 141, M 19, B³ 131, AA⁴ ix 256.
    Change of construction from type A to B: AA⁴ ix 258,
        plate xliii.
    Turrets 17*a, b*: AA⁴ ix 257.
Milecastle 18: M 19, B³ 131, NCH xii 5, AA⁴ ix 257.
    Turret 18*a*: AA⁴ ix 198, 258.
    Turret 18*b*: JRS l 214.
Milecastle 19: M 19, B³ 131, AA⁴ ix, 205, 258; x 98.
    Turrets 19*a, b*: AA⁴ x 98.
Milecastle 20: AA⁴ xiii 259.
Milecastle 21: M 19, B³ 132, AA⁴ xiii 259.

FORT V. HALTONCHESTERS

General accounts: H 105, 142, M 22, B³ 133, NCH xii 468.
Excavation reports:
    Western extension: PSAN⁴ vii 132-4.
    North third of fort: AA⁴ xiv 151-171.
    South-west quarter: AA⁴ xxxvii 177, xxxviii 153; JRS li
        164, lii 164.
Inscription of Hadrian: AA⁴ xiv 161, RIB 1427.
N-W. Baths: Hodgson, *Hist. North.* II iii 316.
Course of Vallum: NCH xii 468.
Corbridge, first- and second-century fort, third- and fourth-
        century supply depot and arsenal: General accounts:
        NCH xii 474 and DUJ xxxiv 144.
    Excavation reports: AA⁴ xv 243, xvii 85, xxi 127, xxviii 152,
        xxx 239, xxxiii 218, xxxvii 20, 59.
    Baths, Red House: AA⁴ xxxvii 85.

Mausoleum, Shorden Brae: AA⁴ xxxix 37.
Corbridge *Lanx:* JRS xxxi 100.

FROM HALTONCHESTERS TO CHESTERS

Milecastle 22: H 143, M 23, B³ 139, AA⁴ viii 317.
    Portgate: PSAN³ ii 283.
    Turrets 22*a, b*: AA⁴ viii 317.
Milecastle 23: H 143, M 24, B³ 139, AA⁴ viii 317.
    Turrets 23*a, b*: OS.
Milecastle 24: H 143, M 24, AA⁴ viii 317.
    Turrets 24*a, b*: AA⁴ viii 317.
Milecastle 25: H 143, M 25, B³ 141, AA⁴ viii 317.
    Turrets 25*a, b*: AA⁴ viii 317.
Milecastle 26: H 143, M 25, B³ 142, AA⁴ viii 317; quarry-wedges
    found, AA⁴ xxxvi 313.
    Turret 26*a*: AA⁴ viii 317.
    Turret 26*b*: AA² ix 234, x 57.
Milecastle 27: M 26, B³ 144, AA⁴ viii 317, AA⁴ xxxi 165.
    Bridge over North Tyne: AA² v 142, vi 80, xvi 328,
    B³ 144; PSAN² ii 178, PSAN³ ii 283.

FORT VI. CHESTERS

General accounts: H 143, M 27, B³ 149.
Principia: PSAN³ iv 134.
Praetorium: AA¹ iii 142.
East gate: AA² vii 171.
South gate: AA² vii 211.
Barracks: AA² xiii 374.
Inscriptions of Antoninus Pius: RIB 1460-1.
Inscriptions of Ulpius Marcellus: RIB 1463-4.
Inscription of Severus: AA⁴ xvi 241, RIB 1462.
Inscriptions of Elagabalus: RIB 1465-6.
Baths: AA⁴ viii 219.
Vicus: AA⁴ xxxvi 228.
Relation of fort to Wall and Vallum: PSAN² ix 307, PSAN³
    ii 284, CW² i 84, iv 240, PSAN³ x 216, AA⁴ xxxvi 230.
Relation of fort to Wall and turret 27*a*: PSAN⁴ x 274, JRS
    xxxvi 134.
Chollerton: PSAN³ iii 322, PSAN³ x 105, NCH iv 263-4.

From Chesters to Carrawburgh

Milecastle 28 : H 144, M 33, B³ 165.
> Turrets 28*a*, *b* : OS.
> Tower Tye temporary camp : AA³ v 262.

Milecastle 29 : H 145, M 33, B³ 166.
> Turret 29*a* : AA² vii 256.
> Turret 29*b* : AA³ ix 56.
> Wall ditch on Limestone Bank : AA³ ix 63.
> Camps on Walwick Fell : AA³ ix 70.

Milecastle 30 : H 145, M 33, B² 167.
> Gaps in Vallum north mound under Military Way : CW²
> xxii 417.
> Turrets 30*a*, *b* : AA³ ix 55.

Milecastle 31 : M 35, B³ 168.

Fort VII. Carrawburgh

General accounts : Gordon, *It. Sept.* 74, H 145, M 34, B³ 169.
Excavations : PSAN² x 161.
Relation of fort to Vallum : CW¹ xiv 415, xv 175; DUJ
> xxix 97, JRS xxv 203.
Inscription of Iulius Severus : RIB 1550.
Baths : Bruce, *The Wall of Hadrian, two lectures* (1874) 17.
Coventina's Well : AA² viii 1, 20 : coins from, *ibid.* 43.
Mithraeum : AA⁴ xxix 1.
Air-photograph of *vicus* : AA⁴ xxxvi 244 pl. xxv 1.
Shrine of the Nymphs : AA⁴ xl 59.
Newbrough fort : PSAN⁴ iv 163, RHW 147.

From Carrawburgh to Housesteads

Milecastle 32 : H 147, M 35, B³ 173.
> Turrets 32*a*, *b*, 33*a* : OS.

Milecastle 33 : AA⁴ xiii 262-3.
> Vallum near 33, M 90.
> Turrets 33*b*-35*b* : JRS xxxviii 84.

Milecastle 34 : H 147, M 35, B³ 174, JRS xxxviii 84.
> Turrets 34*a*, *b* : OS.

Milecastle 35 : H 147, M 37, B³ 176, JRS xxxviii 84.
> Turrets 35*a*, *b* : OS.

The Black Dyke : AA³ xix 121-168.

Milecastle 36: H 147, M 37, JRS xxxvii 168.
  Turret 36*a*: PSAN³ v 66.
Knag Burn Gateway: PSAN¹ i 201, M 92, AA⁴ xiv 172.

FORT VIII. HOUSESTEADS

General accounts: H 148, M 38, B³ 179.
Excavation reports: AA² xxv 193, AA⁴ xxxviii 61, xxxix 279, xl 83.
North gate: PSAN¹ i 256.
East gate: PSAN² ii 204.
West and south gates: AA⁴ xiv 179, 183.
N.E. angle-tower: PSAN³ iv 96.
Inscription of Severus: AA⁴ ix 233, RIB 1612.
Inscription of Diocletian: RIB 1613.
Vicus: AA⁴ ix 226, x 85, xi 185, xii 204, xxxix 301, xl 117.
Baths: AA¹ i 263, PSAN¹ i 52.
Mithraeum: AA¹ i 273, AA² xxv 255, AA⁴ xl 105.
Shrine of Mars Thincsus and the Alaisiagae: AA³ xix 185, AA⁴ xl 121.
Limekiln: PSAN³ iv 96.
Gold rings and coin: AA¹ iv 274.
Relation of fort to turret 36*b*: PSAN⁴ x 274.
Vallum passing the site: AA⁴ ix 225.
Vallum causeway at fort: AA⁴ xi 188.

FROM HOUSESTEADS TO MILKING GAP

Milecastle 37: H 148, M 40, B³ 201, AA¹ iv 269, PSAN¹ i 50; plan, AA⁴ viii 311; Excavation, AA⁴ xi 103.
  Turrets 37*a*, *b*: PSAN³ v 66: OS.
Milecastle 38: AA⁴ xiii 263; *Surtees Soc.* lxxx 134 (inscription).
  Native village, Milking Gap: AA⁴ xv 303.
  Vallum west of Housesteads: CW¹ xv 356.

FORT IX. CHESTERHOLM

General accounts: Hodgson, *Hist. North.* II iii 195; H 148; M 40; Name of fort, AA³ xii 201, B³ 210; AA⁴ viii 182.
Excavations of 1930: AA⁴ viii 182; of 1931, AA⁴ ix 216; of 1932-5, AA⁴ xiii 218.

Principia: AA⁴ xiii 221; Inscription of Caracalla, JRS xxiv 218.
Vicus, plan from air,
Milestones near fort: PSAN³ v 184, RIB 2308.
Crindledykes milestones: AA² xi 130, AA⁴ xvii 116, RIB 2299-2305.
The Thorngrafton coins: AA² iii 269, CW² liv 57.

FROM MILKING GAP TO GREATCHESTERS

Turrets 38*a*, *b*: PSAN³ v 66.
Milecastle 39: M 44, B³ 225, PSAN¹ i 49, AA⁴ xiii 268.
  Turrets 39*a*, *b*: PSAN³ v 66, CW² xiii 306, pl. iv.
  Wall at Steelrig: CW² xiii 307-8, AA⁴ viii, pl. lviii 1.
Milecastle 40: M 44, B³ 227, CW² xiii 318.
  Turrets 40*a*, *b*: OS, JRS xxxvii 168.
Milecastle 41: M 44, B³ 228, JRS xxxvii 168.
  Turrets 41*a*, *b*: OS.
Milecastle 42: AA¹ iv 54, AA⁴ xiii 269.
  Cawfields milestones: AA² ix 211, AA⁴ xvii 117, RIB 2306-7.
  Watermill: PSAN³ iv 167.
  Turret 42*b*: OS.
  Fort at Haltwhistle Burn: AA³ v 213, CW² xiii 379.
  Temporary camps: PSAN³ iii 219, vii 125, AA³ v 259, JRS xxix 202.

FORT X. GREATCHESTERS

General accounts: H 150, Gordon, *It. Sept.* 78, M 45, B³ 232.
Excavations: AA² xxiv 19, PSAN³ ii 287.
Relation to the Wall: AA⁴ ii 197. Relation to milecastle 43: JRS xxx 161, 163-4.
Aqueduct: B² 225, JRS xxxv 80.
Hoard of jewellery: *Archaeologia,* lv 179.
Inscription of Hadrian: B³ 236, RIB 1736.

FROM GREATCHESTERS TO CARVORAN

Vallum at Cockmount: JRS xxx 164.
  Turrets 43*a*, *b*: OS.
Milecastle 44: M 47, B³ 239.
  Turret 44*a*: OS.
  Turret 44*b*: AA² xxiv 13, AA³ ix 56, 69.

Milecastle 45 : M 47, B³ 240.
    Turret 45*a* : AA² ix 234, x 58, AA³ ix 68, CW² xiii 302,
        JRS 1 214.
    Turret 45*b* : AA² ix 234, x 57, AA³ ix 69.
Fell End milestone : AA⁴ x 103, RIB 2309.

FORT XI. CARVORAN

General accounts : H 151, Gordon, *It. Sept.* 79, M 48, B³ 241.
Baths : *Archaeologia,* xxiv 352.
Relics visible 1859 : AA² iv 146.
The Carvoran *modius* : AA³ xiii 85.
Hadrianic inscription : RIB 1808.
Late-Hadrianic Building-records : PSAN⁴ ix 250, RIB 1816, 1818,
    1820.
Cult of Vitiris, Collingwood & Myres, *Roman Britain and the
    English settlements*² (1937), 272, Map IV*c*.
Vallum at Carvoran : AA⁴ xxxi 82.
Teutonic spear-head : AA⁴ xxvi 142.

FROM CARVORAN TO BIRDOSWALD

Milecastle 46 : PSAN³ iv 167.
    Wall and ditch : AA⁴ xxxvii 211.
    Glenwhelt, Chapel Rigg and Crooks camps : M 49.
Milecastle 47 : H 152, M 51, B³ 251, AA⁴ xiii 270.
    Turrets 47*a*, *b* : OS.
Milecastle 48 : H 152, M 53, B³ 251, CW¹ ix 163, CW² xi 390.
    Gilsland, Wall and Vallum : M 90, CW¹ xiii 467, xiv 397,
        CW² xiii 390, xxviii 385.
    Throp fort : CW² xiii 363.
    Turrets 48*a*, *b* : CW² xxvi 429.
    Centurial stones : CW² lv 320, RIB 1859-62.
    Bridge over the Irthing at Willowford : CW² xxvi 429.
Milecastle 49 : M 53, B³ 253, CW¹ xv 352, 374, CW² lvi.
    Vallum here : CW² lvi.
    Turf Wall hence to Birdoswald : CW¹ xv 183, 347, 367.

FORT XII. BIRDOSWALD

General accounts : H 152, Gordon, *It. Sept.* 80, M 54, B³ 253.
Name of fort : CW² xviii 223.

Excavations: 1850, AA[1] iv 63; 1852, *ibid.* 141; 1859, *ibid.* 249; 1896, CW[1] xiv 413; 1897, CW[1] xv 174, 180; 1898, CW[1] xv 345; 1927, CW[2] xxviii 380; 1928, xxix 306; 1929, xxx 169; 1930, xxxi 122; 1931, xxxii 141; 1932, xxxiii 246; 1933, xxxiv 120.

Relation of the fort to turret 49*a* TW: PSAN[4] x 274.

Vallum causeway: CW[2] xxxiii 247.

Inscriptions of Severus and Constantius: CW[2] xxx 199, JRS xix 214; RIB 1909, 1912.

Coin-hoards: CW[2] l 69, liv 56.

Mains Rigg signal-tower: CW[2] xxix 314.

Road from Birdoswald to Bewcastle: CW[1] xiv 196, 420; CW[2] xxii 178, xxiv 110, xxxviii 199.

Robin Hood's Butt signal-tower: CW[2] i 82, xxxiii 241, xxxviii 198.

From Birdoswald to Castlesteads

Wall west of Birdoswald: CW[2] xiii 301.

Turret 49*b*: Hodgson, *Hist. North.* II iii 279, PSAN[1] i 259, CW[2] xiii 303.

Milecastle 50, turrets 50*a*, *b*: CW[2] xiii 312, 307, 309.

Turf Wall, discovery of: CW[1] xiv 186, 399; general account of, JRS xxv 1.

Turf-Wall turret 49*b* TW: CW[2] xxxv 234.

Vallum hereabouts: CW[2] xxxvii 171.

Turf-Wall milecastle 50 TW: CW[2] xxxv 220.

Vallum at milecastle 50 TW: CW[2] xxxvii 166.

Turf-Wall turret 50*a* TW: CW[2] xxxv 234.

Patrol-track on Vallum: CW[2] xxxvii 170.

Turf-Wall turret 50*b* TW: CW[2] xxix 306; xxxv 232.

Milecastle 51: H 153, Gordon, *It. Sept.* 80, M 56, B[3] 266, CW[2] xxviii 384; xxxv 255.

Vallum at milecastle 51: CW[2] xxxvii 158; in original state, CW[3] xxii 398.

Coombe Crag forgery: CW[2] xxx 120.

Lanerton Quarry: Hodgson, *Hist. North.* II iii 440.

Nether Denton fort: CW[2] xxxiv 152, RHW 141.

Stanegate west of this: CW[2] xxxvi 188.

Turrets 51*a*, *b*: CW[2] xxviii 382.

Turret 51*b*: JRS xlix 104.

Milecastle 52: CW² xxxiv 147, xxxv 247; inscriptions, CW² xxxiii 238, xxxvi 1.
    Signal-tower on Pike Hill: CW¹ i 214, CW² xxxii 145, xxxiii 271.
    Turret 52a: CW² xxviii 382, xxxiv 148.
    Boothby, Castle Hill fort: CW² xxxiv 154, RHW 140.
    Stanegate cuttings at Quarry Beck and Pottscleugh: CW² xxxvi 188.

Milecastle 53: CW² xxxiii 267.
    Turret 53a: PSAN¹ i 260; CW² xxxiii 262.
    Turret 53b: CW² xxxiii 270.

Milecastle 54: M 60, B³ 275, CW² xxxiv 144, xxxv 236.
    Clay Wall here: CW² xxxv 244.
    Turret 54a: CW² xxxiv 138.
    Turret 54b: CW² xxxiv 131.

Milecastle 55: M 60, B³ 275, CW² i 8.
    Turret 55a: CW² xxxiv 131.
    Vallum hereabouts: CW² i 77.

Milecastle 56: M 60, B³ 275, CW² i 82, CW² ii 390, iii 346.
    Turret 56b: CW² xxxiv 132.

FORT XIII. CASTLESTEADS

General accounts: H 154, M 61, B³ 276, CW¹ i 204, CW² xxii 198.

Excavation report: CW² xxxiv 159.

Course of Vallum: CW¹ xv 354, CW² ii 385, iii 339.

FROM CASTLESTEADS TO STANWIX

Old Church fort: CW² xxxvi 172.
    Tile and pottery kilns: CW² lxvi.

Milecastle 57: M 61, B³ 276, 285.
    Turret 57a: CW² xxxiv 132.
    Stanegate at Buckjumping: CW² xxxvi 184.

Milecastle 58: M 70, B³ 286.
    Wall hereabouts: *Archaeologia* xi 64.
    Vallum hereabouts: CW² iii 240, M 90.
    Turret 58b: PSAN² vii 221, CW¹ xiii 465.

Milecastle 59: PSAN² vii 221, CW¹ xiii 465.

Milecastle 60 and neighbourhood: B³ 289, M 71, CW¹ xiii 462,
     xiv 191, 393, 405.
     Bleatarn Quarry: CW¹ xiv 405.
     Wetheral Cells Quarry: RIB 1004.
     Gelt Quarry: RIB 1007.
     White Moss: CW¹ xiii 460, xiv 392.
     Watchcross camp: CW² xxxvi 170.
     Stanegate at High Crosby: CW² xxxvi 183.
Milecastle 61: PSAN² vii 220.
Milecastle 62: M 72.
Milecastles 63, 64: M 73.

FORT XIV. STANWIX

H 155, M 74, B³ 290, CW² xxxi 69, xxxii 147.
Excavations, 1940: JRS xxxi 129-30, pl. xii.
Inscription of 167: RIB 2026.
The Vallum: CW² xxxiii 275, xxxiv 155, xxxv 257; JRS *loc.
     cit.*

FROM STANWIX TO BURGH-BY-SANDS

Carlisle, general account: CW² xxiv 95.
Roman name: JRS xxxviii 57.
Early history: CW² xvii 235.
Milecastle 66: RHW 208.
The Wall bridging the Eden: CW² lii 148-153.
Shawk Quarries: Hutchinson, *History of Cumberland,* ii 439.
The Wall passing Carlisle: CW¹ ix 167, CW² xxxii 149.
Grinsdale, Roman camps: M 79, OS AA³ v 262.
Wall at Beaumont: JRS xviii 196.
Milecastle 71: CW² lxi 39.
Wall at the Manor-house: CW² liv 109.
Speergarth Holes, timber foundation of Wall: AA² xii 171,
     CW¹ ix 177.
Wall east of fort: CW² xxiii 8.

FORT XV. BURGH-BY-SANDS

H 156, M 81, B³ 299, CW¹ i 151.
Excavations, 1922: CW² xxiii 3.
Turret 71*b*: CW² lxi 38.
Solway fords: CW² xxxix 152.

From Burgh-by-Sands to Drumburgh

Milecastle 72: CW² lxi 35.
   Turret 72a: CW² lxi 34.
   Turret 72b: CW² lii 15.
Stone and Turf Walls, Watch Hill: CW² xxxv 213.
Milecastle 73: CW² lii 15.
The Wall and Burgh Marsh: CW² lii 16.
Milecastle 76: CW² lxi 31.
Wall east of Drumburgh: CW¹ xvi 92, lxii 60.

Fort XVI. Drumburgh

General accounts: H 157, M 86, B³ 301.
Roman name: RHW 210.
Excavation reports: CW¹ i 209, xvi 81; CW² lii 9.
Harbour: CW² lii 14.
Road to Kirkbride: CW² lii 41.

From Drumburgh to Bowness-on-Solway

Turret 76a: CW² lii 14.
Vallum from Glasson to Bowness: CW² xxxv 214, DUJ xxix 29.
Sunken forest of the Solway: AA¹ ii 117.
Milecastle 78: CW² xxxv 217.
   Turret 78a: CW² lii 14.
   Wall west of Port Carlisle: CW² xxxi 144.
   Wall east of milecastle 79: CW² lii 22.
Milecastle 79: CW² lii 17.
   Turret 79b: CW² xxxv 217.

Bowness-on-Solway

H 157, M 87, B³ 303, CW¹ i 212, CW² xxxi 140.
Vicus: CW² lx 13.
End of the Wall: H 158, M 87, CW² xi 352 (Bainbrigg, 1601).
Kirkbride fort: CW² lxiii 126.

The Cumberland Coast

Beckfoot fort: CW² xxxvi 76; JRS xli, pl. iv, 2 (air-photograph).
Maryport fort: CW² xv 136, xxxvi 85, lviii 63.
Burrow Walls fort: CW² lv 30.

Moresby fort: CW² xlviii 42.
      Inscription of Hadrian: RIB 801.
Milefortlet 1: CW² liv 36, pl. I 1.
Milefortlet 3: CW² xlvii 82, lxii 61.
      Towers 3a, b: CW² xlvii 82.
Milefortlet 4: ibid.
      Towers 4a, b: ibid.
Milefortlet 5: CW² xlvii 85.
Milefortlet 9: CW² liv 36, pl. I 2.
Tower 12b: CW² lvii 22.
Tower 13a: CW² liv 40.
Tower 13b: CW² xxix 146.
Milefortlet 15: CW² lvii 21.
      Tower 15a: CW² liv 36, lvii 18.
Tower 16a: CW² liv 32, lvi 62.
Tower 16b: CW² liv 42.
Tower 20b: CW² lxiii 142.
Milefortlet 21: CW² lxiii 143.
      Tower 21b: CW² lxiii 140.
Milefortlet 22: CW² lxiii 143.
Tower 25b: CW¹ v 124.

THE OUTPOST FORTS

Birrens: Proc. Soc. Ant. Scot. xxx 81-199, lxxii 275-347.
Netherby: Fort-site, CW² liii 6-39.
      Inscriptions, ibid. 20-27.
      Baths, Roy, Military Antiquities of the Romans in North
            Britain pl. xlvi, cf. Archaeologia, lxviii, pl. xxvii; also
            CW² liii 16, fig. 1.
Bewcastle: CW² xxxviii 195-237.
      Bath-house: CW² liv 265, plan 266.
Risingham: AA⁴ xiii 184-196; NCH xv 73, 82, 108, 114, 130.
High Rochester: AA⁴ xiii 171-184; NCH xv 69, 73, 88, 107, 144.

INDEX